World University Library

The World University Library is an international series
of books, each of which has been specially commissioned.
The authors are leading scientists and scholars from all over
the world who, in an age of increasing specialisation, see the
need for a broad, up-to-date presentation of their subject.
The aim is to provide authoritative introductory books for
university students which will be of interest also to the general
reader. The series is published in Britain, France, Germany,
Holland, Italy, Spain, Sweden and the United States.

Frontispiece. View of Florence, about 1500.

S. Dresden

Humanism in the Renaissance

translated from the Dutch by Margaret King

World University Library

McGraw-Hill Book Company
New York Toronto

© S. Dresden 1968
Translation © George Weidenfeld and Nicolson Limited 1968
Library of Congress Catalog Card Number 67–24204
Phototypeset by BAS Printers Limited, Wallop, Hampshire, England
Printed by Officine Grafiche Arnoldo Mondadori, Verona, Italy

Contents

Acknowledgments

The author and publishers would like to thank Miss Diana Souhami who collected the illustrations, and the following sources (the number refers to the page on which the illustration appears): Frontispiece Staatliche Museen zu Berlin; 12, 46, 49, 106, 171 Mansell Collection; 15, 40, 45, 81, 95, 180 British Museum; 17 Alinari, Florence; 20 Bodleian Library, Oxford; 23, 35, 67, 72, 119, 121, 145, 178, 193 British Museum (photo by J.R.Freeman); 25 National Gallery of Art, Washington, D.C.; 29, 41, 65, 99, 105, 217 Scala, Florence; 43 *left* Kunsthistorisches Museum, Vienna; 43 *right*, 146–7 Gabinetto Fotografico Nazionale, Rome; 54, 58, 77, 97, 101 National Gallery, London; 57, 109, 111, 112, 125, 153, 155 Photo Giraudon, Paris; 59 Josephine Powell, Rome; 74 Osterreichische Nationalbibliothek, Vienna; 85 Universitäts-Bibliothek, Erlangen; 92 Foto Oscar Savio, Rome; 98 Royal Library, Windsor (reproduced by Gracious permission of Her Majesty Queen Elizabeth ii); 102–3 Palazzo Ducale, Urbino; 117 Kunstmuseum, Basel; 126, 127 John Rylands Library, Manchester; 139 Bildarchiv Foto Marburg; 143, 199 Hulton Picture Library; 173, 203 Photo Roger Viollet, Paris; 185, National Maritime Museum, London; 187 Science Museum, London; 200 French Government Tourist Office (Photo G. Karquel); 205 Bibliothèque Municipale, Bordeaux (Photo Lacarin); 235 Rijksmuseum, Amsterdam; 236 Castello Sforzesco, Milan.

Preface

At the outset it is just as well to indicate what will *not* be found in the following pages. In the first place no attempt has been made to offer a historical survey of the period concerned. A few dates have been supplied from which to take bearings but there is no question of providing even an approximate historical outline of the diversity of the Italian fifteenth century or the complex development of the French sixteenth century. Quite deliberately, I have confined myself to humanist thought as expressed most potently by some fifteenth-century philosophers, and even so I have dealt specifically only with one or two aspects of this thought. Here too a choice had to be made, and I have decided to pass over the views of many humanists on political or economic matters, and the opinions of a few, even at that date, on social problems. In doing this I am fully aware that I am neglecting an essential part of humanist thought, but, seen in a certain perspective, other problems seemed to me to be of still greater importance. It was the search for some sense of perspective that led me to stress humanist thought in Italy, whereas in sixteenth-century France it is literature which claims the limelight. For if we trace the main streams of Italian thought we shall find them taken up into the French sixteenth century, and to avoid repetition it seemed expedient to show a different aspect of humanism there. Since in both situations we are concerned primarily with works of art or ways of thinking rather than with personalities, I have perforce avoided all biographical detail.

There is no need to emphasise the significance of the period concerned. It is generally accepted that humanism was the movement that brought modern Europe into being. It is true that there are considerable, even essential differences between the humanism of the fifteenth and sixteenth centuries and what is meant by humanism today. And it is equally true that many present-day humanists consider themselves the spiritual heirs of that period. At any rate it is customary all over the world to speak of the humanism of Malraux, Camus, Thomas Mann, and many others. In so far as this involves such concepts as 'human dignity' and 'agnosticism' I not only dispute this use of the term, I consider it quite incorrect. The following pages should make this clear, but they will also show that in other respects common usage has valid antecedents. There would, for example, be nothing against and everything in favour of investigating to what extent the humanist's way of using myths recurs among symbolist poets or in Camus, Sartre and Mann. These poets might also be legitimately studied with regard to humanist irony. The deciphering of humanist allegories in art and thought – to give one final example – often brings to mind modern forms of decoding and the views of Karl Jaspers. All these are important considerations which have not been given the attention due to them. But however we look at the problem, we shall need some understanding of humanism as such, as it manifested itself during the fifteenth and sixteenth centuries. The purpose of this book is to give an introduction to this latter subject.

And indeed, it can be no more than a first introduction. During the last hundred or so years so many studies have been devoted to humanism and the Renaissance, and such a variety of aspects has been investigated from so many points of view that it is now scarcely possible to form a general, let alone a clear, picture. The majority of these studies, moreover, have reached widely divergent – even contradictory – conclusions. From these too a choice had to be made. I have obviously selected those which appeared to me the most reasonable. No informed reader can fail to notice how much I owe to so many of these studies. To name them here, or in the following pages, would be impossible. For this reason then, and also in view of the character of this type of study, no source has been mentioned by name and it is only in a fairly extensive though very selective bibliography that I have tried to show my own leanings. These, I hope, will be more clearly expressed in the usual manner in one or two other publications.

One final observation must be made. It is precisely because of the abundance of published research that it is becoming ever more difficult to define the words 'Renaissance' and 'humanism'. In fact, the question arises whether a general description is possible at all and whether there ever was a Renaissance. The moment has not yet come, however, to discuss this point. And in any case I am by no means convinced that one ought necessarily to start with definitions when dealing with this type of subject. This in itself could lead to more discussions of a general nature and these I shall also avoid. I believe it would be more useful here to consider a few works of that period, find out if they have anything in common, and whether conclusions could be drawn from this. This means that at the start the reader will have to accept a less stringent terminology. It is sometimes a better plan to take the plunge than to hover on the brink debating the temperature of the water.

1 Italian humanism

Pico della Mirandola

In the autumn of 1486 the still youthful Pico della Mirandola had completed and promulgated his nine hundred theses in which he summarised his philosophical ideas. They created an immediate stir, and he then replied by preparing an apologia. Since the public debate, the 'disputation', in which scholars from everywhere could take part, never took place, this address was never given, and it was not published until later. Originally it was simply called *Oratio*; later its title was extended to *Oratio de hominis dignitate*, although this addition was perhaps not quite justified. But it is certainly true that this oration is considered to be *the* manifesto of the Renaissance and of humanism. 'I have read in Arabian books', Pico says, 'that nothing in the world can be found that is more worthy of admiration than man.' We have confirmation of this view, he says, in Hermes Trismegistus and in a number of Persian writers, and even David can be quoted in support. He goes on to mention Moses and Plato (in the dialogue *Timaeus*), and elsewhere in the oration, Pythagoras and his followers, Henoch, the Cabbalists, Mohammed, Zoroaster in the Chaldean oracles, St Paul, and others. It is clear that this work contains a great many names which, in modern thought, look like strange companions, and indeed they do belong to totally different constellations. But in Pico's view, each has an equal right to be produced to support or prove the validity of his ideas. This in itself, even without taking the content into account, poses a problem.

In trying to grasp the substance of Pico's proposition, readers have been confronted by many more problems. One reason for this is that many modern readers have confined themselves to the first few and the best known pages of this oration and have either skipped the rest or considered it of less importance. Right from the beginning Pico emphasises the unique place that man occupies in the world. Man is the focal point in the world, he is at the centre of all that is taking place. When everything has been created and the world is complete, man emerges and God says to him: I have given you no fixed place, no fixed outline, no fixed task, so that

Detail from Cosimo Rosselli's *Miracle of the Sacrament*, 1486. From left to right: Pico, Ficino and Politian.

13

you may undertake any task and occupy whatever place you wish. All else that exists (the rest of creation) is subject to laws that I have ordained. You alone are able to determine what you are. And then Pico exclaims: what generosity of God the Father, what great fortune for man! Who could fail to admire the chameleon that we are!

Many are of the opinion that these few sentences perfectly capture the essence of the Renaissance and how it differs radically from the preceding period called, for reasons of convenience, the Middle Ages. Where God had previously been at the centre, Man now takes this place. There would seem to have been a complete *volte face*. Such an interpretation, however, is seriously open to question. Rather than comment on this in general terms at this stage, it is preferable to give a short summary of the remainder of Pico's address. If we are free, Pico continues, to make our own choice, there is only one aim that we should pursue. Let us despise all that is worldly, as many have told us to do. Let us seek what is heavenly and above the world and in nothing shall we be less than angels. By killing all that is physical we shall attain pure spirituality and we shall find heavenly rest and peace, perhaps while we are still here on earth. The mysteries of many religions contain veiled allusions to this possibility. It is not only the Mosaic and Christian mysteries that point in this direction, but Socrates' ecstasy, described by Plato in the *Phaedrus*. The Muses and Apollo also say as much. Philosophy can unravel these mysterious and often hermetic pronouncements and this is precisely why Pico says that he was driven to the study of

Julius Caesar depicted as the founder of
Florence, by Maso Finiguerra. Many fourteenth-
and fifteenth-century humanists were historians,
who were inspired by patriotic motives to discover
Roman origins however spurious.

philosophy. It is for that reason, and for that reason alone,
that he wished to launch a discussion.

There are then several aspects of this manifesto of the
Renaissance – for that is undoubtedly what it is – that would
seem curious to us: there is a curious mixture of philosophical
and religious motifs which, to our way of thinking, should be
separated. Great emphasis is laid on the specific nature of
man who is free and able to change, but who should use
this freedom to aspire after God. These views are finally
substantiated with all manner of widely diverging pronouncements. All this is typical of humanist thought and
so it is up to us to find out how this structure of thought
developed and what laws it obeys, however strange they
may seem to us. Even for a rough sketch of this configura-
tion we need to see where it sprang from and what its
potential was. We might, for instance, start by asking whether
Pico had in fact read all of his numerous sources – though
there can be little doubt that he had – and in what language
he read them.

The study of Greek

It has been asserted that without the remarkable interest
in Greek and the resultant upsurge in knowledge of it
during the fifteenth century, there would have been no
Renaissance. According to this view, the Middle Ages took
their bearings only from Latin culture, and Greek authors
were read only in Latin translations. Formulated like this,
the contrast is undoubtedly too sharp; even if knowledge of

FLOREZIA.

IVLIVS CAESAR

Dante and the city of Florence, from a fresco
by Domenico di Michelino, 1465.
Humanism, and especially Florentine humanism,
was greatly influenced by Dante, who in turn
was inspired by Graeco-Roman culture.

Greek was slight and readers of Greek few and far between, instances of both could be quoted even in the Middle Ages. In the first place it ought to be borne in mind that Sicily and Southern Italy, not merely for reasons of geographical proximity but also by a long-standing tradition going right back to antiquity, were steeped in Greek culture. Several monasteries, moreover, maintained a Greek tradition as a result of which some knowledge of Greek was carried to western countries as far as Ireland. One of the people who profited by this Greek tradition was Charlemagne, in his negotiations with eastern rulers, and it is not unlikely that he himself had some command of the language. Finally there are two further reasons why Greek could not have been completely neglected during the Middle Ages: the influence of the Greek Church Fathers and the existence of the Greek Empire, where the ancient tradition was never lost.

Increasing connections with the Greek East encouraged a deepening of interest as early as the beginning of the fifteenth century, which soon swelled to a considerable enthusiasm. In 1395 Chrysoloras, accompanied by another Greek scholar, arrived in Venice and after a few years – at the instigation of Salutati – was teaching his own tongue in Florence. More important, Salutati's successor at the city's chancery, Leonardo Bruni, set about making Greek texts available, which meant translating them into Latin. This marks the appearance of the first important humanist translations from the Greek, some of which provided more accurate and subtle translations of texts than were then available in earlier Latin versions.

In Florence then, knowledge of Greek became fairly widespread, and it must have created a great deal of interest when the council initiated in Ferrara was moved there. One of the most important subjects to be discussed was the reunification of Eastern and Western Christianity. This brought many Greek theologians to Florence and here they found a climate extremely favourable to the language and culture of ancient Greece, in which people were prepared to adopt and assimilate a great deal. Among this group of theologians Plethon and his disciple Bessarion should be mentioned by name, since they were instrumental in increasing the knowledge of Greek and, even more important, in drawing attention to a number of Greek texts which were until then, if not unknown, at any rate completely neglected.

The search for manuscripts

Before going into this any further it is as well to point out that although these texts had been virtually ignored during the earlier Middle Ages, they had nevertheless been preserved during these hundreds of years. The humanists are often represented as being the first to show a scholarly interest in these manuscripts, as opposed to the medieval monks and scholars who, it is said, showed much less concern. Had this been entirely the case these manuscripts would never have survived until well into the fifteenth century. In our desire to credit the Renaissance with its due we should not completely strip the Middle Ages of theirs. The difference is rather that the humanists showed a fresh and, one might say, unprejudiced interest in ancient texts and that they had an almost insatiable curiosity about unknown manuscripts. In fact there was what one could call a boom in manuscripts; scholars made their way to monasteries – the most promising hunting grounds – in far distant regions to see if there was anything of interest there, and that included anything that could be called ancient. Princes, merchants, wealthy citizens, all sent people out to search for manuscripts, since any manuscript would enhance their library, whether or not it could or would ever be read.

The earliest important discoveries had already been made more than a century earlier. The manuscript of the poems of Catullus, which came to light as early as 1295, could be considered to be the first of these. Petrarch was in possession of manuscripts – although he was unable to read them – of Plato and Homer, and in this way, one after another, many Greek and Roman writers were rediscovered; Cicero became known almost in his entirety, and he was followed by Livy, Tacitus and many others. For one of the most famous descriptions of the enthusiasm aroused by the manuscripts we have the record of Poggio Bracciolini who was present, as apostolic secretary, at the Council of Constance. He used his spare time to see what he could find in the monastery of St Gallen and he informed his friend Guarino, who had visited Greece with a similar end in view, how fortune had favoured him: he had discovered writings of Quintilian and Cicero. Later on in the fifteenth century Bisticci, a bookseller, reported on the enthusiasm with which men like Pope Nicholas v, Lorenzo de' Medici, Federico

MARCI TVLLII CICERONIS ORATIO PRO Q. ROSCIO AMERINO INCIPIT FELICITER.

CREDO EGO VOS IVDICES MIRARI QVID SIT QVOD CVM TOT summi oratores hominesque nobilissimi sedeant ego potissimum surrexerim qui neque etate neque ingenio neque auctoritate sim cum his qui sedeant comparandus. Omnes enim hi quos uidetis adesse in hac causa iniuriam nouo scelere conflatam putant oportere defendi defendere ipsi propter iniquitatem temporum non audent. Ita fit ut adsint propterea quod officium secuntur taceant aut idcirco quia periculum metuunt. Quid ergo? audacissimus ego ex omnibus? minime. At tanto officiosior q̄ ceteri? ne istius quidem laudis ita sum cupidus ut aliis eam prereptam uelim. Que me igitur res preter ceteros impulit ut causam sex. rosci reciperem? quia si quis istorum dixisset quos uidetis adesse in quibus summa auctoritas est atque amplitudo. Si uerbum de re p. fecisset id quod in hac causa fieri necesse est multo plura dixisse q̄ dixisset putaretur. Ego etiam si omnia que dicenda sunt libere dixero nequaq̄ tamen similiter oratio mea exire atque in uulgus emanare poterit. Deinde quod ceterorum neque dictum obscurum potest esse propter nobilitatem et amplitudinem neque temere dicto concedi propter etatem et prudentiam. Ego siquid liberius dixero uel occultum esse propter quod non dum ad rem p. accessi uel ignosci adolescentie mee poterit tametsi non modo ignoscendi ratio uerum etiam cognoscendi consuetudo iam de ciuitate sublata est. Accedit illa quoque causa quod a ceteris fortasse ita petitum sit ut dicerent ut utrumuis saluo officio se facere posse arbitrarentur. A me aut hi contenderunt qui apud me et amicitia et beneficiis plurimum possint quorum ego neque beniuolentiam erga me ignorare nec auctoritatem aspernari nec uoluntatem negligere debeam. His de causis ego huic cause patronus exstiti non electus unus qui maximo ingenio sed relictus ex omnibus qui minimo periculo possem dicere. Neque uti satis firmo presidio defensus Sex. roscius uerum uti ne omnino desertus esset. Forsitan que

Page from Cicero's *Orations*, unsigned. The
scribe is identifiable as Piero Strozzi, a
Florentine priest who copied a great many
manuscripts between 1443 and 1483 or later.

d'Urbino and several foreigners wished their orders to be
carried out. Intellectual snobbery certainly had its part in
this, but it is also true that this kind of fashion was instrumental in promoting learning and led to results that could
not possibly have been foreseen. For instance, a cult which
owed its origins mainly to scholars and philosophers
supplied them with more texts and facilities than they could
have envisaged. Prince Lorenzo benefited greatly from the
efforts and industry of all those concerned with the arts and
sciences in Florence, and he learned of the latest develop-
ments more easily and sooner than if he had had to find out
for himself. Conversely other people gained the advantage of
all the facilities that he, in his position, could provide.
In the same way it was Lorenzo's grandfather, Cosimo de'
Medici, who, after the arrival of Plethon and Bessarion, may
have set Florentine humanism on its ultimate course.

Marsilio Ficino (1433 - 1499)

Of middle-class parentage himself, Cosimo had made an
incalculable fortune for his family and had made them the
actual rulers of Florence. Because of his great interest in
the arts many scholars and artists were at his disposal, one
of whom was Marsilio Ficino. Born in 1433 Ficino began
his studies in Florence and continued in Bologna, that is to
say he attended courses following the traditional medieval
curriculum and even wrote one or two essays in the ap-
proved convention. As yet he had no knowledge of Greek,
but he had read a great deal in the available translations,

especially Plato. This information reached Cosimo, who had long been hoping to stimulate a greater interest in this philosopher. This transpired to be a turning point in Ficino's life and, indeed, led to an event that was going to determine the future of Florentine learning. For it was in 1459 that Ficino embarked on a study of Greek and began his life's work, translating and annotating Plato and Platonic philosophers, and writing original works which are, nevertheless, closely related to the thinking of the ancient philosopher he so greatly admired. The translation of a few hymns, ascribed to Orpheus, was followed in 1463 by the *Poimandres* (or 'Shepherd of Men'), one of a series of writings believed to reveal the secret doctrine of a fabulous godhead, Hermes Trismegistus, for which reason they were termed 'hermetic' literature. In the quiet atmosphere of his country house at Careggi, presented to him by Cosimo, he was now making translations of Plato's own works. The following selection may give some impression of the enormous quantity of work produced by Ficino (as it was by other humanists in other fields): translations of Plato's complete works and commentaries on Plato and the works of Plotinus, the last of the great Platonic scholars of the third century AD; translations and commentaries on the works of Plotinus' disciples, Porphyry, Proclus, Iamblichus and others, who between them worked out the neo-Platonic philosophy; translations of Dionysius the Areopagite, a medieval mystic writer; and finally his own works, *On the Christian Religion*, *Platonic Theology: Concerning the Immortality of the Soul*, and so on. All this was accomplished in the course of forty

Title page of Ficino's *Platonic Theology: Concerning the Immortality of the Soul*, 1487. This was Ficino's principal philosophic work, based largely on Plato's *Phaedo*. Ficino had begun his Greek studies in 1459, and soon embarked on a complete new translation of Plato which did much to promote Platonic study, and the study of philosophy in general. The translation was printed in Florence in 1483–4.

M.D.XXV.

years – Ficino died in 1499 – and by that time, Plato's complete works, the writings of neo-Platonic thinkers, hermetic literature and many other treatises were available not only to the Florentine élite but to the entire civilised world.

In his country house Ficino used to collect a circle of friends, and under his guidance the ideas of Plato, the revered master, were discussed in free and easy conversation. With others, whom he could not reach in this way, he maintained regular contact by means of extensive correspondence. And thus his ideas spread, and Platonism became *the* Renaissance philosophy, or at least it became much better and more completely known than before.

Platonism

If it is often said that the Renaissance and humanism are due to a revival of Greek, it is also claimed that they originate in a renewed interest in Plato. The Middle Ages were said to have confined themselves to Aristotle, whose influence and significance were declining rapidly in the course of the fifteenth century, thereby allowing Platonism free play. This is indeed a neat and tidy explanation but reality is here much more complex and less obvious. This is not the place to go into this in detail; it will be sufficient to mention one or two points within this development that are illustrative of the situation in the fifteenth century.

During the twelfth and the thirteenth century, medieval thinkers had access to a great deal of Aristotle's work in

Verrocchio's terracotta bust
of Lorenzo de' Medici (1449–92).

<u>Latin translation, but these translations were not from the Greek originals</u>. In previous centuries Arabs in particular had been interested in Aristotle, and this gave rise to translations, not only in Arabic but also in Syrian and in Hebrew and it was from these languages, in Spain, that Aristotle's works were translated into Latin. It is obvious that his ideas did not benefit from this treatment and in some cases there was little left of his original thought. Nevertheless his works, and particularly Averroes' commentaries, created a great stir. Thomas Aquinas, for instance, succeeded in producing a magnificent synthesis of Aristotelian and Christian concepts and the resultant fusion makes it almost impossible to separate the two. Scholasticism embroidered upon this and developed a refined system of reasoning which was accepted as the philosophy of the schools throughout the remainder of the Middle Ages. No doubt this system degenerated into a collection of subtleties and quibbles. Nevertheless the system was still thriving in the fifteenth century.

So much so, in fact, that <u>Averroism in particular blossomed anew. This form of Aristotelianism was taught at the University of Padua by Pomponazzi and by his pupils after him</u>, albeit in a free and individual interpretation. <u>Averroes exercised a considerable influence during the Middle Ages</u>, even though his ideas seemed scarcely compatible with Christian belief. Pomponazzi expressly accepted the Church's dogmas and then ignored them completely. This led to double standards of truth; on the one hand there was the Church's teaching, on the other there was the development of independent philosophical thinking. As a result, Pomponazzi's ideas were thought to reveal the contradiction in both and the beginning of rationalism.

Certainly French thinking and scientific development during the sixteenth century were to interpret the Paduan school in this sense, and here we have the ground for the argument that humanism contained a concealed or camouflaged form of atheism. It is questionable, however, whether this kind of argument could be made to fit the historical facts.

It is quite certain that Florentine humanism took a stand against these ideas, and it was, of course, Averroes' philosophy which Petrarch so fiercely opposed in the fourteenth century. In this, and in his zeal for the true faith, he showed the tendencies of the times he lived in. In his argument he quoted Paul and Augustine, but also Plato and especially Cicero who, partly because of this, was to have a lasting influence on the humanists. Indeed, it was through Cicero's writings that the Middle Ages had gained some knowledge of Plato's ideas, for Cicero provided an outline and a synopsis of them so that, even if indirectly, he was not entirely unknown. In the fourth century moreover, Chalcidius had produced an incomplete translation of the dialogue *Timaeus*, which was accompanied by an extensive commentary. Here again, a translation was the direct cause of immense aftereffects, since it modified the concept of the universe held by medieval thinkers and writers and, certainly to no lesser degree, by the humanists too. Plato then, was known directly only from this dialogue and one or two others, and even

Detail of Raphael's *School of Athens*, 1508.
Plato points to the heavens while
Aristotle is more concerned with earthly
affairs. In the foreground is a melancholic
figure variously described as a Greek
philosopher and as Michelangelo.

then only in translation and through commentaries with, inevitably, their individual interpretations. Nonetheless, Platonism played a definite part during the Middle Ages, and after the twelfth century it had its heyday in Chartres, under teachers like Bernard of Chartres, his pupil John of Salisbury and others.

If Platonic thought was developing fairly consistently along these lines, if fragmentarily and possibly in a garbled form, there were other currents of Platonism which are much more difficult to follow. Various forms of Platonic thought crop up in the most widely separated fields, and quite early on in the Middle Ages they are connected with the most unexpected phenomena. One such was the need felt by Christianity during its first few centuries for a philosophical basis or at any rate a philosophical affirmation of its faith. In disputes with agnostics and pagans it was necessary to fight them with their own weapons. Moreover, every educated Christian's schooling had evolved from and was determined by the Graeco-Roman system that had been fashionable for centuries. Augustine is a classic example of this, for he was converted to Christianity from a pagan upbringing in which he had been steeped in neo-Platonic thought which he later worked over and adapted. And even in his opposition to these ideas their influence is noticeable, and what is true of him is also more or less true of others. The teaching of the Church Fathers, for instance, acquired a great deal of (neo-)Platonism on its way through the centuries.

Elsewhere a similar marriage took place in the writings

of Dionysius the Areopagite. During the Middle Ages and the Renaissance it was generally accepted that this author was none other than the St Dionysius whom St Paul had met in Athens. In fact nothing is known about this writer, but he was probably a monk who wrote his mystical treatises in Greek in the sixth century if not before, and who was markedly influenced by neo-Platonism. They had a very great impact on the West as well as on the East (from a Latin translation in the ninth century) and they largely determined the character of Catholic mysticism. Hence right from the start the most intense religious experiences are not devoid of neo-Platonic ideas, and since Dionysius' work was so widely read, it is not surprising that the humanists should deduce that St Paul's faith did not widely, let alone fundamentally, deviate from the principles of Greek thought.

Finally, there is one more instance of an extraordinary fusion of ideas likewise due to an erroneous dating which once again very much affects humanism. The hermetic writings were thought to contain a divine being's primeval revelation of wisdom and religious affirmations made to one or two initiates who, in their turn and in secrecy, were allowed to instruct their disciples in the doctrine. But all these treatises date in fact from the second century AD, and they too mainly derive from the neo-Platonic world of ideas, even though the revelations were ascribed to an Egyptian god Thot, whom the Greeks identified with Hermes. Nor is this to be wondered at in the melting-pot of philosophical ideas and religious experiences which the Roman empire was in those days. What is extraordinary about this hermetic literature is that religious motifs can scarcely be differentiated from philosophical ones: they are one and the same. The initiated strive after a religious ideal along a philosophical route, not forgetting the magic elements in all their profusion and intensity. Because of their diversity of origin – some of them are written in Latin, others in Greek – and also because of the peculiar character of the mystical experiences, these treatises cannot be said to form a closed system. They do contain a 'doctrine', however, and their appeal is that this doctrine is secret, though to the initiated an infallible way towards eternal happiness.

For the humanists, the manuscript that was brought from Macedonia to Florence was a revelation in every sense of the word. Cosimo commissioned Ficino to interrupt his work on the Plato translations so as to translate Hermes Trismegistus into Latin. This Ficino did in a very short time and Cosimo was able to read the book just before he died in 1464.

The primary significance of all this for humanism is that the available sources, all apparently of different origins, nevertheless all revealed the same thought and projected the same religio-philosophical world of ideas and, despite unmistakable differences, obviously contained one and the same revelation. That this is indeed so, is, as we now know, due to the fact that the mysticism of the pseudo-Dionysius, the hermetic writings and the many other writings not mentioned here, are indeed closely bound up with neo-Platonism. Humanist thought, therefore, is in certain respects based on an imperfect knowledge of historical truth. This, of course, in no way belittles what the humanists did with the material once it was theirs.

The Cabbala

Platonism then, was not unknown in the Middle Ages but it was certainly enriched and extended in the fifteenth century. Another element ought to be noted which, though originally outside the framework of pre-humanist thought, was yet drawn into it, cropping up here and there throughout the Middle Ages and, apart from a few admittedly important exceptions, affecting only a special circle. In adopting this element humanism was not modernising and revitalising in its own way a long-standing tradition. Here it was as if the humanists were discovering a new aspect of culture. Hebrew was naturally of great importance in Jewish circles, but outside these circles it understandably attracted less attention. An exception to this is the contact that was maintained in theological circles between Jewish and non-Jewish scholars in Spain, the south of France and elsewhere. This contact was intensified and extended more and more during the fifteenth century and there are various reasons for this. One of them is, of course, that in the Renaissance view every scholar ought to know, in addition to Latin, both Greek so as to read the New Testament, and Hebrew in order to read the Old Testament in its original tongue. Among those greatly interested in Hebrew were Giles of Viterbo, Pico della Mirandola and later Johannes Reuchlin, a genuine scholar and the greatest Hebraist of them all. Their circumstances were somewhat unusual. Giles of Viterbo, a cardinal, was the protector of Jewish scholars. Pico attended their classes. Jews collaborated in their publications with humanists, but at the same time the Jewish religion was of course rejected, and the Talmud in particular was held in contempt. This, however, was not the fate of other works written in Hebrew (or Aramaic), for which admiration increased rapidly. From the beginning of the thirteenth century onwards cabbalistic influences were clearly discernible in Jewish circles and towards the end of that century the *Zohar* (or 'Book of Illumination'), the cabbalistic work *par excellence*, was compiled in Spain. On the authority of Moses de León, who probably wrote it himself, a certain rabbi Simeon ben Jochai is named as the author who talks, with his son and pupils, about everything that occurs in heaven and on earth. Moreover, this rabbi is supposed to have set down only what is claimed to be the essential teaching and wisdom of the Jews, handed down by Moses by word of mouth to the initiated on Mount Sinai. This supposition greatly appealed to humanist thinking and it was eagerly accepted in all seriousness.

Without going into the sometimes fantastic, sometimes very profound and always fascinating ideas of the Cabbala, the point of importance here is that the whole work is infused with speculations on language and words – the mystical contemplations being centred round the Divine Name. And when we remember that in Hebrew each letter also has a numerical value, we can expect no restraint on the reconstruction of casual evidence and interpretation,

Celestial scripture, from Athanasius Kircher's
Oedipus Aegypticus, with a description
(on the upper part of the page) of cabbalistic
signs, the forms of which could only be
revealed to initiates. On the lower
part of the page is the Hebrew alphabet.

far-reaching observation and questionable magic. All this
undoubtedly appealed to the humanists, though some went
further than others, so that whereas the Cabbala had much
less fascination for Ficino than for Pico, later Paracelsus,
Agrippa von Nettesheim (Cornelius Agrippa) and others
were to become its devoted adherents. Pico is more inclined
to confine himself to theoretical considerations, but in one
of his nine hundred theses he goes so far as to say that there
is no clearer evidence for the divinity of Christ than is
provided in magic art and the Cabbala. Using a cabbalistic
method in the *Heptaplus* he demonstrates his point: by
several mutations of the letters of the first word of the Old
Testament it can be read in different ways, thereby pro-
ducing a number of Hebrew words. When these are translated into Latin it will be clear to everyone that this very
first word contains one of the most important Catholic
dogmas. It is not our concern here to consider how learning
could have benefited from this kind of manipulation. But it
is our concern to realise that this kind of treatment was of
great importance to Pico and gave strong support to his
ideas. For only if we do our part by being prepared to
accept this, can we hope to appreciate the directions humanist
thought was taking. For instance the fact, mentioned earlier,
that Pico made scarcely any distinction between philosophical and religious themes, transpires to be no new
phenomenon but merely one aspect of a long-standing
tradition. Nor is it surprising that he quotes all kinds of
names from very different spheres as being authorities in
one and the same field. For this is the direction in which

non habet, præter arbitrium & autoritatem inſtituentis, illius inquam, qui huiuſmodi literarum inſtituendarum & cõſecrandarum acceperit poteſta‑ tem, cuiuſmodi apud diuerſas nationes & religionum ſectas plures fuerunt ſacrorum antiſtites, quorum inſtituta ad nos non peruenerunt, præter pau‑ ca quædam ſparſim aut per fragmenta ab autoribus tradita. Ex horum itaq; characterum genere ſunt, quos notat Petrus Apponus ab Honorio Theba‑ no traditos, quorum figura eſt talis ad noſtrum alphabetum relata:

Alius characterizandi modus, à Cabaliſtis traditus.
Caput   X X X.

Pud Hebræos plures characterum inuenio modos, quorũ unus eſt antiquiſſimus, ſcriptura uidelicet antiqua, qua uſi ſunt Mo‑ ſes & prophetæ, cuius forma nemini temere reuelanda eſt: nam quibus hodie utuntur literis, ab Eſdra inſtitutæ ſunt. Eſt etiam apud eos ſcriptura quam uocant cœleſtem, quia inter ſydera collocatam & figuratam oſtendunt, non ſecus atq; cæteri aſtrologi ſignorum imagines è ſtellarum lineamentis educunt. Eſt etiam quam uocant ſcripturam Mala‑ chim uel Melachim, hoc eſt angelorum ſiue regalem: & eſt alia quã uocant tranſitus fluuii, & horum omnium characteres & figuræ tales ſunt.

Scriptura Cœleſtis

| Theth | Cheth. | Zain. | Vau. | He. | Daleth. | Gimel. | Beth. | Aleph. |

| Zade | Pe | Ain | Samech | Nun | Mem | Lamed | Caph | Iod |

| Tau | Shin | Res | Kuff |

Scriptura Malachim

humanist thought was moving and it might well be wise to deal with this now in so far as it concerns one of the most difficult and the most disputed aspects, religion.

Docta religio

Viewing the situation schematically – which is imperative here – we see that philosophy and theology were kept separate in Padua by Pomponazzi and others. Religious dogmas might be accepted but they were always set aside, thereby allowing an almost independent advance in philosophy and scientific thinking. In Florence and elsewhere, on the other hand, no less bold attempts were made to marry religion (and that of course meant Catholicism) and philosophy in a harmonious relationship. The results of these efforts may seem more strange to us than what was happening in Padua, since these ideas were destined to have a long and prosperous future, whereas many would say that the Florentine school came to nothing. I do not agree, and even if it were true, it can scarcely detract from the importance, integrity and intensity of their efforts.

In his *Oration* then, Pico cites many very varying authorities. Nor is this the only instance of this kind of method. He does this all the time. In a description of his conversation with Savonarola the names of Moses, Pythagoras, Hermes, Zoroaster and Salon are mentioned in one breath. Orpheus and Plato happen to be missing in this case, but they can be found elsewhere. Ficino shows a similar tendency, for although the accumulation of names is often less obvious in works of such length, they are there nevertheless. The same can be said of many of their contemporaries and disciples. And they all use the same method of reasoning and adducing evidence.

As one example out of many I choose a Lazzarelli dialogue because he, being one of the minor writers and thinkers, exaggerates this tendency. In order to demonstrate the validity of a secret and mysterious revelation he argues as follows:

Hermes told us ... Abraham gives us the same instructions in *Sepher Izira* (= *Sepher Yetzira*, a cabbalistic work) ... Plato mentions it in *Phaedrus* ..., and so does Philo, but superior to them all is the message of the true Messiah, our Lord Jesus Christ ... and a *Genesis* commentary agrees with this ... but (as was pointed out before) Jesus Christ revealed this profound mystery ...

It does not concern us here which particular revelation is being referred to – what matters in this context is that in Lazzarelli's opinion they all say the same thing, and that Christ says it better and more categorically than the others.

There is absolute unanimity: Plato is Moses speaking Greek. In fact, this view goes back to the first centuries AD and like others similar to it, having figured less prominently during the Middle Ages, it was taken up by the humanists in all seriousness and with utter conviction. Our first reaction is likely to be that this kind of statement can only be accepted as a figure of speech, and we can demonstrate this by referring to a linguistic problem. Whereas in Latin, which has no articles, the statement reads: Plato is Greek Moses, the modern languages must of necessity add one of the articles: Plato is *a* or *the* Greek Moses. This simple fact is not without significance, for the insertion of this article adds such a comparative force to the words that it is all but impossible to read them as an equation. And quite apart from this, how could anyone ever dream of making Plato and Moses into the same person? And did the humanists really do this? The last question is easily answered: they did not do so. For them, too, Plato was not the same person as Moses, and yet he was. What was stated by the former as the most profound truth about man and the world, is exactly what was contained in the words of the latter. To us this unanimity is paradoxical, perhaps even ludicrous. For the humanists it was essentially a given fact, scientifically justified and by no means contradictory.

And it is for this reason that the humanists exerted themselves to achieve a synthesis of religions in a spirit of the purest and noblest idealism. The greatly admired Cardinal Nicholas of Cusa devoted several treatises to this subject as early as the middle of the fifteenth century. In his essay *De pace fidei* ('On the Peace of the Faith'), a truly ecumenical document, representatives of the different religions come to the agreed conclusion that they all, in fact, profess one religion, a mitigated Catholicism in which, for instance, the sacraments play a less important part. A similar ideal can be found in Ficino, Pico, and most of the others. It is not by chance that terms like 'peace', 'concord', 'marrying', 'joining', 'harmonising', 'reconciling', recur with such regularity among these writers. They are expressions of their firm conviction that the possibilities are there and that it is up to philosophy to see them fulfilled. If they are successful in this, then the divine soul will ascend to its origin and return to its fatherland. When one considers that this mystical experience was for many the ultimate good, it will no longer be strange or difficult to understand that Pico was drawn to Savonarola's radical views and that he led an ascetic life. There is no reason to see this as an interruption in the course of his development. Although there are other versions of the event, Politian's moving description of Lorenzo's death seems to me symbolic. The prince and patron of humanism was facing death with complete humility and surrender. He wished to see Pico but later Savonarola also entered the room and Lorenzo asked for his blessing. At that time there was no conflict between humanism and the Church – the humanists for their part were believers, while we are liable to take an *a posteriori* view of the Church in those days, looking at it through Protestant eyes.

It is only by accepting this complete unity as fundamental that everything that appears to us paradoxical and even blasphemous can be seen to have developed naturally. One example will suffice, and again, for the same reason as before, it is taken from the same work by Lazzarelli. Indeed, its title alone, *Christ's Chalice, Hermes' Cauldron*, is sufficient to set modern minds wondering what on earth is afoot! Is it not a little unlikely that a work with this title could come within the scope of the Church's dogmas? Are there not concealed allusions to paganism here, going right beyond the bounds of Catholicism? I am putting the questions, although I have already given my answer. If

humanist piety is to be understood at all, it must be realised
that this kind of attitude is not only possible but actually
basic. It is true that Lazzarelli ventures far and yet, apart
from a charge of indulging in magic, he scarcely encountered
any opposition from the ecclesiastical authorities. This
book, at any rate, abounds in examples of this unity we are
concerned with. Lazzarelli is a Christian and is not ashamed
of being a Hermetic at the same time. So when, at the end
of an argument, a sentence reads: 'Therefore I will praise
Christ Jesus under the name of Poimandres', this should
really no longer surprise us. It is an expression of sincere,
Christian piety, admittedly of a particular kind which we

Left Maso Finiguerra's engraving of Hermes Trismegistus. Hermes holds out a manikin before an astonished warrior. A well-known passage in a Hermetic work (*Asclepius* 23–4) attributes to the highest type of man the power of bringing statues to life. *Below* A mosaic picture of Hermes by Giovani di Stefano, inlaid in the pavement of Siena cathedral.

Right Reverse of a Politian medal, by Niccolo Fiorentino. Politian was one of the greatest scholars of the time and the first to explain the subtleties of Latin poetry. *Far right* Reverse of a Pico medal, also by Niccolo Fiorentino. The inscription must be interpreted in the light of Ficino's philosophy of love. For Pico too, the universe was an ordered whole, bound together by love.

must learn to understand, but which we should not discount from the start as being impossible, dishonest or ridiculous. Never for a moment did it occur to the humanists that they were wrenching texts out of their context or distorting them, or that they were reconciling what we now consider irreconcilable. They were convinced – and their own reasoning and insights were their proof – that the unity was there, that all the ancient theologians and philosophers had said the same. The revelations granted to Orpheus, Pythagoras, Plato, Moses, Christ, and others, were essentially all the same, even if they were formulated in different ways.

To assume that these religious convictions were opposed to what is generally termed scholasticism would also be quite incorrect and entirely contrary to humanist intentions. It is true that Petrarch adopts this kind of attitude towards the Averroists, but it is for falsifying if not completely stifling the truly religious experience that he attacks them. Certainly Ficino has the greatest admiration for Thomas Aquinas, and Pico dedicates a large number of his theses to scholastics and quotes them frequently. And when the opportunity occurs he ardently defends them. In fact, how could it be otherwise since in this striving for unity nothing was to be excluded. And in this respect it is impossible to make a distinction between humanism and scholasticism, or more generally, between Renaissance and Middle Ages. These distinctions are solely the result of a construction of the historian's own making.

Similarly, it would be incorrect to surmise that the humanists were aware of a radical distinction between

Aristotle and Plato. Except in Padua, where the former received almost exclusive attention from many scholars who were thereby continuing and extending a medieval tradition, Aristotle retained his place despite the fervent admiration for Plato. For Plato, such attributes as 'divine', 'heavenly' were revived; meanwhile Aristotle remained 'the philosopher'. In the dedication to his friend, Politian, in his discourse *De ente et uno*, ('On Being and the One'), Pico says that all those who claim to see any distinction, let alone antithesis, between the two philosophers, will find him their opponent. Earlier on he had written to a friend about the course of his studies and how he had passed from Aristotle to Plato. Not that he should be called disloyal for that reason, he continues, for although the words they use could hardly be more dissimilar, it would be difficult to find greater agreement than theirs in their substance. Here again, we find the humanist indulging in his characteristic pursuit of looking to the philosopher's work to reveal the unity which he assumes to exist.

It will be clear by now why little or no distinction was made between, for instance, philosophy and theology. To

Maso Finiguerra's *Linus and Museus*,
about 1460. Along with Orpheus and Arion,
Linus and Museus formed part of a mythological
series of inspired poets and musicians,
at once civilising heroes and poets.

our minds this seems strange and very hard to understand because of our tendency towards specialisation, which first arose during the sixteenth century and which has been progressing ever since, resulting in the present-day maxim that every branch of scholarship has its own aims, its own methods and its own objectives. And we have gone such a long way in that direction – as perhaps we should – that we have lost sight of the common ground which nevertheless exists between these branches of scholarship and their objectives. This tendency could already be discerned in certain medieval circles when philosophy and theology began to be more sharply divided. In this respect then, humanism was not continuing the work begun by some medieval scholars, nor was it, on the other hand, heralding the modern age. On the contrary, like Dante – whom they so greatly admired – the humanists adhered to an ancient view that philosophy, theology, poetry, and so on formed an unbreakable unity. Orpheus is perhaps the best example of this; he is pre-eminently the divine singer, being not only a poet but also a prophet inspired by the gods, revealing sacred truths, and is thus a philosopher. Another example was the philosopher Pythagoras whose person had long been surrounded by legend. He was considered to have founded a religious sect, which is by no means improbable. There is, of course, no question here of mixing religion and philosophy, since in ancient Greece the two were simply indistinguishable. The same could be said for Zoroaster, but it is much harder to justify this idea where Moses and the Old Testament prophets were concerned. Nevertheless, fifteenth-century humanists

LINVS·MVSICO·EPOETA

MVSEVS·MVSICO·EPOETA

Luca della Robbia's *Pythagoras*
or *Arithmetic*, from the tower of
the cathedral in Florence.

47

continued to hold this view. For them every thinker of importance was essentially proclaiming religious truths, and conversely, no prophet or religious leader ever lived who was not a philosopher. In their opinion true philosophy inevitably leads to faith, indeed, philosophy is faith, faith is philosophy. This is what turns philosophy into a pious, religious activity, into what was called the *pia philosophia*; religion is intrinsically philosophical, so that it will be *docta religio* ('learned religion'), disclosing an ancient, often secret, revelation to be deciphered in the works of the philosophers.

Seen in this context, a title as surprising as *Platonic Theology* becomes quite meaningful. There is no question of a contradiction between Plato and Catholicism, nor is it at all strange when Ficino declares that no one can come to Christ except by means of Plato. It is the philosopher's task to demonstrate the harmony and concord between Platonic thought, that is to say, thinking at its best, and Catholicism. Pico's *Heptaplus* is a philosophic explanation of the creation of the world, and incredible though it may seem to us, there appears to be no difference between his findings and what was revealed by Moses to the Jews and what is described in Genesis. If this text is read according to the standards of Pico and the other humanists, the conclusions can be seen to be final and indisputable.

This did not mean that philosophy confirmed religious dogmas and definitions of faith. It was rather a question of philosophy proving itself to be in agreement with what had been taught by and known in religion all along. In general this kind of problem arose as soon as there was mention of Christian philosophy and whether this was a feasible concept at all. These were urgent problems during the Middle Ages and they still are in the study of medieval philosophy. In an entirely individual and original form, the same difficulties arise, quite independently, in the ideas of a contemporary philosopher, Karl Jaspers. And in my view it is no accident that the humanists were not troubled by problems of this kind. They simply could not exist for them since philosophy and religion were not only intertwined, they were one and the same thing. To many humanists, the philosophic treatise was also a religious tract: it was impossible to write the one, to write it properly at any rate, without also writing the other. So it will not be surprising if, in future, whenever the discussion turns to the humanists' attitude to the world, their religious convictions again come to the fore. For many humanists the concept of the divine is undoubtedly religious, and for some of them most certainly the result of a deep, if not ecstatic experience, and it is no less philosophic for that. This is due to the fact that they were reading the ancient texts and discovering the unity in them. Nevertheless, we are still left with the question how and where they managed to find this unity in the given texts.

The revival of antiquity

Quite often the Renaissance and humanism are 'defined' as a revival of Graeco-Roman art and philosophy. This is an attractively neat description, but it suggests answers to a

Detail of Botticelli's *Punishment of Korah,*
Dathan and Abiram. A biblical story is
re-enacted before the Arch of Constantine.

number of questions which are scarcely being asked, or at any rate, carries a number of implications that cannot just be ignored. A revival of antiquity? That is all very well, but in that case antiquity had apparently died. Is this so? And if so, when did it happen? Traditionally the answer to this question is that at the beginning of the Middle Ages (whenever that may be) Graeco-Roman culture was on the decline, and after becoming less and less important it re-emerged in the Renaissance. Such a distinction has currency, but it is not necessarily true to the facts. As we noticed earlier in connection with other phenomena, this distinction, however deeply entrenched, should be challenged. The vexed question of the dating of the Middle Ages will not be my concern here. Nor will I attempt to call on the plentiful available evidence of Greek and Latin influences at that time. Instead I will confine myself to naming a few of the salient phenomena of importance to the period we are concerned with here.

During the many centuries comprising the Middle Ages there was an almost uninterrupted confrontation with ancient culture and – to a much lesser extent – with Graeco-Roman art. This means that medieval Christendom was faced with the difficulty of determining which reactions to this pagan culture to accept and which ideas and art forms to reject. The problem proved to be so great that they were never really able, willing, or courageous enough to take a definite decision in this matter, so that we can observe dissident points of view existing cheek by jowl, as in Jerome and Bernard of Clairvaux, ranging from an almost complete acceptance of ancient civilisation to an entire rejection of it.

But antiquity as such was always a live issue in medieval culture.

While we cannot then shrug this element off in the Middle Ages, no more can we point to a sudden and universal acclaim of the ancients during the Renaissance. In the first place ancient culture extended over many centuries from Homer to Plotinus (two relatively arbitrary limits) and it was not known in its entirety. The humanists elucidated some of its aspects with greater clarity and alacrity than others. And there were elements in this thought (especially where Epicurus was concerned) which most of them rejected with horror or endeavoured to Christianise as much as possible. So that there is no question of a complete rejection on the one hand or a complete acceptance on the other.

Where then does the distinction between the Middle Ages and the Renaissance lie? Or is there no distinction at all? Even if there were one, it would still be extremely difficult, if not impossible, to express it in general terms. Perhaps the best we can do is to begin by stating two extreme points of view, if only because they demonstrate how the problem ought to be put. Lorenzo Valla, an important humanist, said that Latin had not been spoken for centuries (during the period we call the Middle Ages) and that no one could any longer understand what he was reading in Latin. Some present-day scholars, on the other hand, argue that it was primarily the humanists who were responsible for Latin becoming a dead language. What is one to make of these theories? Surely we are faced with a double paradox here? On the one hand we are asked to believe that medieval

scholars, all of whom were writing in Latin, had no knowledge of this language, and on the other hand, the *revival*
of Latin is supposed to mean its *death*. To take the first
point: the historical evidence is quite clear and irrefutable
that Valla was wrong. There remains the possibility that
his interpretation of these facts was different from ours,
since he saw them in a different light. To us Latin can only
be Latin, whether one is referring to the classical writers
like Cicero, Tacitus and Virgil, or the medieval writers like
Thomas Aquinas, or the humanists. They all wrote in Latin
and that would seem to be the end of it. Not quite the end,
though, certainly not for Valla in whose opinion medieval
Latin was a kind of Latin but not as true and thoroughbred as
it should be. Small wonder that his words quoted earlier occur
in the preface of a work dedicated to the *Elegantiae*! According to him, medieval Latin showed little resemblance
to the pure and exact language which he wished to re-
habilitate; it was no longer Latin.

Although Valla's comment concerns only Latin, it is in
fact typical of a change in attitude towards the whole of
ancient culture. This attitude is best expressed by the concept
of *imitatio*, which was to play such an important part in all
humanist thinking and right up to the latter half of the
eighteenth century. Throughout that time this concept was
often modified, and there have been so many and such
varied interpretations of it that it is becoming increasingly
difficult to understand what was meant by it. There is no
doubt that *imitatio* already figured prominently in Roman
culture, which strove to imitate Greek culture in many

respects and, by so doing, to acquire it. It is remarkable, however, that the Middle Ages, apart from one or two inevitable exceptions, paid little attention to it and it is only in humanism that *imitatio* comes right into its own again. The reason for this is probably that the Middle Ages simply did not feel the need to imitate ancient literature and art; it is true that they were aware of the significance of Graeco-Roman antiquity and they stood in awe of it, but they never saw this antiquity as something uniquely great, with its own characteristics and its own laws.

With a kind of childlike simplicity the medieval artist, without more ado, appropriated what appealed to him. From his point of view ancient civilisation was more or less the beginning of the Middle Ages. He did not appreciate its peculiar value, nor could he be expected to, for he lacked any kind of historical perspective. There was a complete change, however, in the Renaissance, when the ancients became an example in their own right, to be considered as an entity as well as individually, so that Graeco-Roman art and philosophical ideas became truly exemplary, giving rise to that reverential admiration which is so typical of the Renaissance. We can put it this way: the humanists regarded antiquity as remote in time (whatever was old had a special appeal for them) but near to them in thought, whereas the Middle Ages were closer in time but in many respects far removed from their mentality. On this analysis, Valla was right. Medieval scholars and artists in Italy did, of course, *live* in closer proximity to antiquity than later generations. The people of Rome spent every day of their lives among the

ruins of the ancient city. And that is exactly why no one was aware of these many remains as being relics of a different culture, of another world. They were part of their very lives and so they treated them as they pleased. The humanists, however, rediscovering a sense of the uniqueness and significance of antiquity, set the fashion in the fifteenth century for excavating and for a scientific interest in Roman buildings. Not surprisingly, trading houses dealing in antiques sprang up, and there is an anecdote about one of the first of Michelangelo's works which is symbolic of the

Lorenzo Lotto's portrait of Andrea Odoni, 1527.
Odoni was both collector and scholar, and deeply
interested in the newly-recovered sculpture and coins
of the ancient world. So great was the fashionable
and commercial value of these works that the
'finds' were sometimes of dubious authenticity.

spirit of the age, even if the story is apocryphal. After making a sleeping *Amor* he is said to have hidden the sculpture under the ground, so that it would emerge as an antique! All this is proof of the exemplary and unique character of antiquity but it also shows that its culture was put on a pedestal and evaluated in isolation. The humanists no longer took it for granted as part of their daily lives; it used to have a life of its own and it was their earnest desire to imitate this earlier existence and to fit it, with its autonomous significance, into the contemporary cultural situation. The essential change in the attitude to the classical era came about through the simple transition from familiarity with the common-or-garden in the Middle Ages to respect for the special and the remote in the Renaissance. To argue that in this process the humanists were mummifying antiquity is, in my opinion, a gross overstatement. But it is certainly true to say that the tradition of what was meant by ancient culture underwent a fundamental change.

In the uninterrupted classical tradition throughout the Middle Ages all pagan elements, where they could not be Christianised, were rejected and certain other elements, because proscribed, went, as it were, into hiding (and more of them later), but against this the need was felt to keep alive the fame of the ancient Roman Empire politically as well as culturally and to incorporate it into the glory of the Holy See. And Rome, whether in her ancient or her new splendour, was the crown of this endeavour. And so, not unnaturally, this was the place through the centuries for the emulation of classical Roman life. Politically, for

Theology being taught at the Sorbonne,
fifteenth century. In the Middle Ages,
Paris had been considered the new Athens
but by the fifteenth century Florence
had won that honour. Intellectual life in
Paris was dominated by scholasticism.

instance, they made attempts from time to time to revive
in concrete form the ancient Roman Republic, even though
these attempts were not always equally serious and appear
to the modern world to have been little more than make-
believe. Some circles adopted Latin names, Latin customs,
and pressed, if only half-heartedly, for the acceptance of a
republican administration. Nor was this genuine attempt
to incorporate the old into the existing situation, which was
certainly one of Charlemagne's ideals, confined to political
imitation. Throughout the centuries there had been a desire
to project not only the Roman Empire but the whole of
ancient civilisation on to the present. In the Middle Ages,
during the heyday of the university there, Paris was regarded
as the new Athens. Later on, a great humanist like Cristoforo
Landino was to demand this honour for Florence, while
Paris shared its glory, and French humanists of the sixteenth
century envisaged something of the kind for Lyon. Even if
it is here again difficult to distinguish between total and
spiritual revival, I would venture to suggest that this re-
introduction of ancient culture, which could be described
as a form of 'nationalism', tended to be visualised in concrete
terms. In the end all these attempts – Cola di Rienzo's
became the best known – came to nothing, but afterwards
they were considered to have heralded the Renaissance and
humanism, although there appears to be no justification for
this view. For humanism is concerned not so much with
reviving the ancient world as with absorbing the *spirit* of the
ancient culture. Not that they entirely lost sight of a concrete
revival of antiquity in its actual form. Physical antiquity

was and remained remote; it was its spirit, its tone and general appeal that were near enough to be recaptured.

We have already seen that there had been no lack of attempts of this kind during the Middle Ages. And any distinction we try to make between Renaissance and Middle Ages is only relative and tends to evaporate. In a sense, things were a good deal simpler for the medieval artist and scholar; there were no problems at all for him in this respect. Entirely unhampered, he appropriated whatever he found and turned it into something contemporary. The Renaissance artist recognised and appreciated the peculiar nature of ancient culture, saw each work as a complete entity to be imitated, and more, incorporated it into his own time and in accordance with his own world of ideas. It would seem, therefore, that the tensions between the various elements (which were not really considered to be essentially different) and the harmonious resolution of them in the work of art was much more apparent during the Renaissance than it

had been. Any humanist or Renaissance work can be cited as an example of this, and I will confine myself to one subject so as to consider this in some detail.

The difference between pantheism, which was the linch-pin of classical mythology, and the Christian monotheistic doctrine, can only be described as radical and insuperable. And the fact that we are not surprised that this mythology played an important part during the Renaissance suggests that we have made up our minds about the pagan nature of Renaissance thought and art. What may be surprising is that this was a continuation of a strong medieval tradition. What is more, it does not seem at all unlikely that the Roman myths, not to mention the Greek, were known chiefly

Left The return of Odysseus, by Pintoricchio.
Below Scene from the *Aeneid* by Apollonio
di Giovanni. The heroes of Greek and Roman
literature are seen here in fifteenth-century dress.

through medieval sources. Encyclopaedic works like those by Isidore of Seville (sixth to seventh century) and Arabanus Maurus (eighth to ninth century), both widely read and of great importance in the medieval world of ideas, contain long dissertations on mythology. Special treatises were devoted to this subject, even by early Christians: by Servius (fourth century), Martianus Capella (fourth to fifth century) and especially by Fulgentius (fifth century). The interest continued undiminished during the later Middle Ages. John of Salisbury and Alain of Lille may be named among the many who contributed to a fairly wide stream of mythological literature that penetrated well into the Renaissance. Boccaccio, known mainly to us as the author of the

Decameron, was certainly no less well-known at the time for his work *The Genealogy of the Pagan Gods*, which was a summary of virtually all that had been said before, and which became the Renaissance artist's handbook.

We may accept that there had been this great interest for centuries, but it remains incongruous to us for all that. And it will be more surprising still when we examine the means they had at their disposal to justify ancient mythology in Christian eyes. Yet this was quite possible during the Middle Ages and the Renaissance – and in this respect there is little difference between the two – and it was done by reading in a certain way, which was considered to be the only correct way for centuries. It was thought that the ancient myths should be read *allegorically*, and that they only revealed their true meaning after they had been stripped of all kinds of inessential wrappings. Or rather, the texts were thought not only to convey the obvious but to point to something different, something more profound and more secret, which did not appear on first sight. In this way each text could be read at different levels of understanding and and on deeper acquaintance it would prove to contain something quite different from what was at first surmised. Odysseus' return voyage, described in Homer's *Odyssey*, could also represent the search of the soul for its native land. Through this kind of interpretation Hercules could become Christ, and so could Apollo and others. And is the *Song of Solomon* merely an epithalamium? There is no doubt that this kind of interpretation is now considered highly dangerous: reading into the text what one wants to find there – a serious form of subjective manipulation, etc. And it is equally certain that we have by no means outgrown this method and in many fields we are – even if subconsciously – persisting in it, while some forms of poetry even deliberately do so, and quite rightly. At any rate, allegorisation permeates all medieval and Renaissance thinking and it has very deep roots. Even in antiquity the Stoics made it their task to elicit the actual meaning of the Greek myths and fables in this way. Nowadays we recognise that they were overlaying mythology with morality and hence we are inclined to draw the conclusion that their only concern was to preserve the often candid stories by resorting to allegory. This is by no means so. There is no question of expedience or necessity, nor should we think that they did not take it seriously. For centuries, to allegorise was the most excellent and perfect way to read, the only way which did justice to all that the text had to say. It was not long before a biblical tradition developed which, in harmony with the existing Stoic and other ancient traditions, cropped up everywhere. In this way, as for instance in the reading of cabbalistic literature, they penetrate 'the bark of the language'. Each word, each sentence, is allowed to retain its immediate meaning but it can also be interpreted otherwise. Most of the humanists cultivated this as an ingenious pastime, to our minds sometimes sterile, often quasi-profound and always unscholarly, but it was without doubt at that time the accepted method of reading. And this method either prompted or stimulated a striving towards unity. In any case the two are closely interrelated.

Allegory

Pico's *Heptaplus* is in many ways one of the most striking examples of this method. Pico distinguishes between four different levels of interpretation and systematically explains how the biblical account of the creation of the world can be read at these four levels, so that each time his interpretation is a perfect rendering of the way in which these four worlds have been organised. The humanists had developed a cosmic view scarcely deviating from the medieval one and directly or indirectly resulting from Chalcidius' commentaries and translation. The whole of neo-Platonism saw a continuity from creator to all that had been created. One can best imagine this, as they did in antiquity, as a chain extending from the creator to the lowest of his creatures and thus linking everything. This concept and variants of it constantly recur in Pico, in Ficino's *Platonic Theology*, and in many other works. In God, the creator of everything, there exists unity, perfection and perfect rest. And without attempting to go into the extremely complicated philosophical and theological ramifications, we can at least say that this perfect immobility, just because it is perfect and hence outpouring in love, creates as it flows, and expands in the process. This is how the heavenly spheres were created, with their hierarchy of angels (one of Dionysius the Areopagite's concepts) and these were equated with Plato's system of thought. According to Pico, God himself is utterly indescribable and inexpressible, an idea originating in the 'negative theology' of the Middle Ages and from Nicholas of Cusa. In essence, the realm of the angels cannot really be fathomed either, but it is slightly easier to imagine, for the angels are lower, they are spirit but they are present in myriad numbers. God is spirit and God is one. At the head of this divine realm God has placed the spirit of the universe, sometimes identified with the sun. The moon forms the transition from the divine realm of the ether to the universe of the air in which we also live. This latter world is dominated by multiplicity, mobility and materiality. These three then, God, the heavenly world and the material world, are in contact with each other and, as many would have it, embrace one another. The lowest point of the heavenly sphere, the home of the angels who are involved with the material world and man, forms the direct transition to the world in which we live. Fallen angels will literally fall from the heavenly world into the material one and will become demons. And there were some who maintained that this was how ancient gods and heroes continued their existence. There is obviously no movement in God, who is utter immobility. But there is an ordered and, naturally, also perfect mobility in the heavenly world, which is generally thought to be circular and thus always returning to itself. Like all movement, this perfect movement produces sound, which is obviously perfect and, according to the views of the Pythagoreans, of the purest harmony. One of the most exalted, if perhaps erroneous, notions revived first by Cicero and others and particularly by the humanists, was this harmony of the spheres, to be found again much later in Shakespeare's works. This perfect, harmonious movement could also be acquired by the human soul during its ascent along the chain of its entire existence. But otherwise the material world was subject to an increasingly disordered instability, even though there was still the link with all that was on a higher level, so that the higher could be found on the lower and the lower in the heavenly. The earth presented yet another hierarchy: mere existence (stones, for instance), existence coupled with growth (plants), existence with growth and sensations (animals) and finally man. Man occupied a special place, but before exploring this further, mention ought to be made of the four elements in the material world which could be connected in different ways: earth, water, air and fire, fire being the lightest of all. Bearing in mind that any of these four could be linked with the contrasts hot-cold and wet-dry, it will be obvious that there was room here for all kinds of combinations. It was commonly held that these were important not only in the creation of the world but also, for instance, in medicine where they continued to play a part. All the various mixtures of the elements in hot, cold, or moist conditions determined the physical and psychical conditions of man. Words like 'humour', 'temperament' and 'melancholy' are reminders of all this to this day.

The place of man

Of greater importance still was the place occupied by man. Even from this brief survey, which is far from complete and which scarcely does justice to the systematic thought and

Detail from Crivelli's *Coronation of the Virgin*. The art of music was accorded special reverence for it echoed the harmony of the spheres.

Illustration from Bovillus' *Liber de intellectu*, 1509.
The hierarchy of earthly existence is demonstrated twice. First,
man's natural potential is greater than that of the other 'kingdoms'
because he has the power of reason. Secondly, by an act of the
intelligence he can choose to tread the paths of virtue, but if he
does not so choose he will not fulfil his potential.

ingenuity of the many writers concerned, it will have
become clear that the creation, starting from God, came
about step by step, in descending order, and was literally a
degradation, in which the earth and everything earthly were
truly the lowest point. But man, as Pico had already pointed
out, was a creature apart. On the material side he was composed of all the various elements and subject to change. But at
the same time he was a soul and between the two was the spirit,
no longer possessing the matter of the body but not yet
able to claim the total immateriality of the soul. Since man
was blessed with reason, he was a unique creature and in his
Oration Pico at once drew attention to this fact. He was
unique for, as the Bible says, he had been created after
God's image. Paradoxically therefore, man combined within
himself both the material element, inherent in the inhabitants
of the lowest point of creation, and the exceptional greatness
of the only being made in the likeness of the Creator. In the
first instance then, this concept, often seen as one of the
most typical features of the Renaissance, was a direct result
of biblical, orthodox piety. This implies however, that on
this point too there can be no radical or absolute contrast
between humanism and the Middle Ages. But during the
fifteenth century the current image of the human situation
was being enriched or at any rate made more complex by
similar ideas derived from neo-Platonism and hermetic and
cabbalistic writings. Plato himself indicates that man must
acquire the likeness of a god, that he must immortalise
himself so that he can become an observer of divine activity.
It is as if man is a god, an earthly god. It was considered

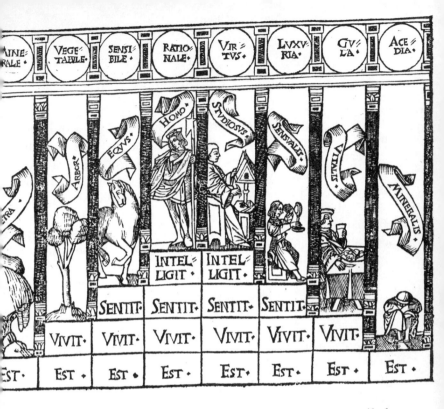

that all these Platonic terms could easily be reconciled with Christian concepts like Son of God, God's children, and so on. They did, in fact, think that these Christian concepts were concerned with the same things. Plato's descriptions, explanations like those in Cicero's widely read and deeply admired *Scipio's Dream*, obscure treatises from among the hermetic writings, they were all directed towards the aim summed up in the Bible by the image of God.

Without surrendering much of what we would call 'orthodoxy', humanist thought placed man at the centre of creation. He was the orbital point, the centre, the actual link between all that had been created. He belonged to the lower and even the lowest element, he could rise to within the heavenly sphere and perhaps even higher to God himself. After the three worlds he was a fourth world in his own right. Pico della Mirandola had some doubts about this definition: in his opinion (and many of his followers agreed with him) there was really no need to devise a fourth world. In man the three worlds converged, he embraced them and contained them, as it were. He was a world in miniature, a microcosmos (just as, conversely, the world was seen as a huge person).

Although it would seem that opinions like these need not necessarily be at variance with the Christian faith, many people today find this hard to accept. But are we then not concerned here with the burning question of human dignity? Is this not a specifically Renaissance emphasis which would have been unacceptable to the preceding centuries when God, and only God, was central? The last question has already been answered, and the first question scarcely presents any problem. Pico's famous *Oration*, as we have seen at the beginning of the chapter, certainly contains definite statements about this. The question is whether they refer to what is nowadays understood by human dignity (human, that is to say, as opposed to divine dignity). There is no doubt that this runs completely counter to the philosopher's intentions. He was convinced that true human dignity could only be found in the blissful state of proximity to God. *On the Dignity of Man*, the title given to his *Oration*, is only suspect in so far as it is far too often misunderstood. In this, and in almost all his other writings, this dignity is only mentioned in conjunction with an almost mystical union with God and the divine. That is why we should be extremely cautious when we interpret a famous and much quoted sentence, often considered as the Renaissance slogan: 'Who would not admire this changeable chameleon?' Pico is assumed to have contrasted God's motionless perfection, recumbent upon itself, in which the Middle Ages (and the humanists!) believed, with the greatness of that which is changeable, of man. But he never fails to emphasise that man has been given this mutability with one single aim in view. It is true that man can degenerate to the animal, but just because of his essential worthiness he can renew himself, as St Paul says, and he can return to the divine. Only then will he find the rest, peace, unity and bliss of the divine life (and these words are just as typical of Pico and humanist thinking as all those referring to changeableness). That is why, says Pico, it is of the utmost importance that man, placed as he is at the centre of the world, should in his turn look to Christ, the perfect mediator.

All this does not mean that humanist thought does not in any way differ from previous thinking. For although we have found that a straight contrast between the two gives a far too rigid account of the facts as they really are, they are, nevertheless, not completely alike. An essential and, at the same time, rather elusive distinction in their respective views of man is the striking difference in tone. Pico's works express an enthusiastic and youthful *élan*, a firm intention to fathom the world and in this process to allot man a special place. Ficino's tone is a little more dispassionate and sedate, but he and his contemporaries show essentially the same spirit, and the same earnest desire to understand what man is. As a result the same facts and ideas which existed both in the Middle Ages and in the Renaissance were elucidated in different ways and acquired a different relationship. If the humanists displayed a particular interest in man's potentialities and in his creative power, this by no means implied that this interest had not been there until then. For one thing the products of medieval civilisation utterly belie this. It is true, however, that the Renaissance in all its art forms stressed the nature and the possibilities of this free activity.

Astrology

Man's potential reveals itself in various fields. Some of them cannot fail to cause astonishment by their imperfect statement of the problem. If one starts from the premise frequently adopted, that compared to medieval thinking, humanism is a definite breakthrough where modern rationalism blossomed for the first time, then it becomes very hard to understand why it is that astrology and magic were so very important in the fifteenth century and continued to be for a long time afterwards. If however, we accept the system of creation outlined above, then both these will find their natural, and even necessary places in it. One can no longer even imagine the structure without them, since it is this chain, running right through creation and connecting everything with anything, that offers the possibility of influencing one thing through another. And it is obviously to man, orbital centre of the world, that an opportunity of this kind is given first of all.

Astrology is ancient and it has been at all times, as it still is today, of great importance to many people. During the first centuries AD it blossomed anew. It is one of the many aspects of neo-Platonism; its function in hermetism should certainly not be underrated and it emerged once again in the Cabbala. The later Middle Ages and in particular the Renaissance added material from Arabic sources. One of these is a 'book of magic' called *Picatrix*, which is anonymous but was almost certainly commissioned by King Alfonso of Spain during the thirteenth century, or at least translated from Arabic into Latin at his request. It has been ascribed to all kinds of people, some important, others less so, but the real author remains unknown since Picatrix is nothing more than an incorrect Latin rendering of the Arabic name Bukratis, in its turn a faulty rendering of the Greek name Hippocrates. I am giving these details since they provide an illustration of the complicated pattern of cultural development and also because they demonstrate once again what an immense influence translations of this kind can have within a certain civilisation. That the humanists were interested in this and other astrological or magical writings, is at one and the same time both comprehensible and incomprehensible in the traditional scheme: incomprehensible, since they are supposed to have been rationalists, and indeed this interest is less noticeable in Paduan circles; understandable, since their attitude as regards Christian

commandments is thought to have been less rigid, so that they could openly display their interest in this pagan 'science'. Whatever the case may have been, it is a fact that the great majority occupied themselves in one way or another with the mysterious relationships that appeared to exist between the constellations, earthly events and life. These relationships may be obscure, but they can be investigated, thereby introducing a kind of intellectual astrology. One can, perhaps ought to, go further than that; the starry system determines what takes place on earth (the astrologer's premise); conversely, man might be able to bring his influence to bear on this determinism, introducing magic. And although this is no new phenomenon, the Renaissance

The Astrologer, by Giulio Campagnola, 1509. The
humanists' interest in astrology and magic would seem
at odds with their more rationalistic attitudes,
but they were concerned with the whole of creation,
an integral part of which were the relationships of
the stars to the earth and to human life.

produced all manner of theoretical astrological views, the
realisation of which sometimes turned out to be rather
timid in practice. It also produced real sorcerers, going
through the world as miracle-men, swindlers who appeared
to be honest but deceived themselves most of all, and finally
others who can only be called charlatans.

How could this rampant growth of astrology square with
Christianity? There are various possibilities here. The
most important connections can undoubtedly be traced back
to the various observations on the subject from some of the
Church Fathers. Initially the Catholic Church took up an
extremely cautious attitude towards astrology, first because
here it was up against a deeply rooted superstition, and
secondly because even in the Epiphany story and other
biblical accounts there might be some elements of astrology.
St Augustine for one was not opposed to astrology in so
far as it concerned nature. But man, being to some extent
free, could not possibily be subject to the restrictive regularity of planetary movement. Astrology, therefore, could not be
applicable to man. Thomas Aquinas had similar views and,
as we know, his opinions came to carry much weight. Even
in the seventeenth century his arguments were still being
quoted as conclusive evidence by Campanella, a particularly interesting astrologer and miracle-worker, whose
views on this subject were really a last off-shoot of the
Renaissance. If then, in the fifteenth century, Pico wrote an
extensive work attacking astrology, this is not because he
was so 'modern' and because his position was so close to
ours, but because he too, like Augustine and Thomas

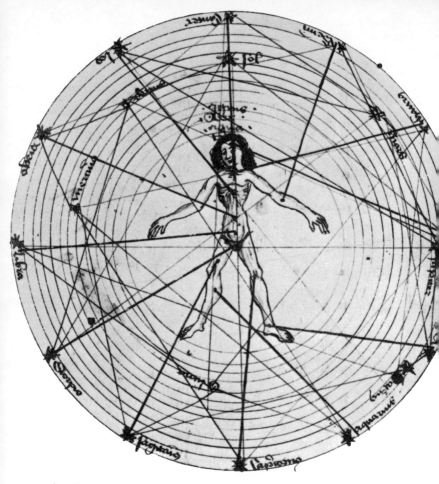

Aquinas, wished to safeguard human freedom. His arguments are really none other than those of his admired examples.

Like Ficino he distinguished between two kinds of magic and astrology, one of which was good and useful, the other demonic. Ficino, more inclined to astrological reflections and practices than Pico, naturally confined himself only to the

Man as a microcosm. The Christian doctrine
that God created man in his own image led
to the view of man as the microcosm. Conversely,
the universe was sometimes portrayed as a
huge man. Here, the signs of the zodiac
correspond to different parts of the human body.

first. He carried this so far, however, that he was considered
to have shown a way to penetrate the heavenly spheres. And
we would certainly be quite wrong to look upon these ideas,
so very dear to Ficino, as a trivial and naïve pastime. For
him and for many like him they were undoubtedly part of
what we would now call natural philosophy. They were an
indispensable part of it and had an organic place within the
whole concept of relationships. Since everything was inter-
connected and since there were sympathies throughout the
entire creation, it was obvious that the existing affinities
could be systematised. There was, for instance, a connection
betwen planets and human nature. People who had a definite
connection with Jupiter in the hour of their birth, had a
jovial nature (an idea retained to this day). A connection with
Saturn led to melancholy. But stones, especially precious
stones, also had their place in this scheme of things, like
everything else. Hence the popularity of amulets and the
like. Astrological medicine had its place too, of course, for
since the disease was obviously symptomatic of a disturbance
of the humours, medicine would try and restore the balance,
i.e. the necessary harmony, by the use of formulae, herbs
appertaining to certain planets, and a host of such devices.

This aspect of humanist thought has been discussed in
some detail because it has not previously received the
attention due to it. It also seems to be coming back into
favour today. Nevertheless we must remember that astrology
had a detrimental influence on progressive thought, then as
now. Of much greater significance to us is undoubtedly the
value which humanist thought attached to existence as such,

St Jerome from a painting of Jan van Eyck's, now lost, by Antonello da Messina, born 1430. As opposed to many scholastics, the humanists recognised the importance of the Church Fathers, particularly of Jerome, translator of the Vulgate. Erasmus, who edited Jerome for Froben in 1516, preferred him to all the other Fathers (Luther preferred Augustine).

and to what could be expected or required of man. In order to understand this we must start from a much more sober and precise viewpoint than is offered by astrology and magic.

Philology

In the first half of the fifteenth century especially, and hence among the earliest humanists, there was a desire for authentic texts written in pure Latin. And as we have seen this resulted in earlier translations being replaced by new and better ones, and accurate editions of familiar works as well as totally unknown works began to appear. In fact, the return to the classics was also determined and certainly reinforced by a desire to emulate the Latin language in all its perfection, and so this revival depended on a better knowledge of classical Latin. It has already been pointed out that in Valla's opinion true Latin had fallen into disuse. Moreover Valla was one of the first to investigate the authenticity of the available sources by sound philosophical methods. One particular source presented a considerable problem: should biblical texts be submitted to a critical examination? For centuries the Bible had been the divinely inspired book and not an iota in it was to be changed. It was not that the original Hebrew and Greek retained much of their importance, but the Latin Vulgate had an absolute power and validity that was inviolate. By returning to a better or at any rate a different Latin, and especially because of the primacy which the original languages were regaining, the humanists began to reflect on the different languages

in which the Bible was written, on the meaning of the words, on the content, and especially on the context. Valla never published his *Notes on the New Testament*. The reason for this is not entirely clear, although we might suppose that he was aware of the risks involved in his attempts at textual criticism and wanted to guard against them. This does not, however, tally with the fact that many knew his work in manuscript, that even Pope Nicholas V was in agreement with its purport, as were Cardinal Nicholas of Cusa and others. Whatever the reason, the work was not published until the sixteenth century, by Erasmus. By comparing a number of New Testament manuscripts, Valla discovered a number of incorrect renderings in the Vulgate. But this does not mean that he questioned the theological interpretations. Valla had always maintained that he was not correcting Holy Writ but a translation. Besides, he was not concerned with the truth of the Gospel, but with the correctness of the Latin. Nowadays we may find it extremely difficult to separate the two; we might even suspect Valla of hypocrisy. There is certainly no justification for this at all since textual criticism was only in its infancy, and at the time it seemed perfectly possible to make this distinction without there being any further religious implications.

This was certainly possible for Valla, since he was one of the greatest representatives of an ambition so characteristic of the first humanists (for the whole of humanism, as some would have it). Valla's object was Latin in its true glory. He was obviously also concerned with what was written in Latin but this can be considered of secondary importance only. First and foremost he was fascinated by the way in which the content was formulated. Since Roman times there had been an increasingly elaborate system of rules for proper speech and the correct use of language. Together, these rules made up rhetoric, the doctrine of accurate formulation, and from the days of Cicero onwards many grammarians and others had incorporated them in the official curricula of schools, both in Roman times and in the Middle Ages. Lorenzo Valla's work is undoubtedly a stage in this development and like him, the first humanists paid the utmost attention to what may be termed eloquence. The term easily leads to confusion, but before going into this any further, here is one example from Valla's work on the correct usage of Latin. Suppressed by the barbarism of the Middle Ages, Latin, he said, must be recaptured in its essential form. Maintaining the military analogy he continues by referring to the territory regained by one, or the city liberated by another. But the most important of all is he who returns the lost standard to his native country, thereby restoring his country's honour. As it stands, this is a fortunate simile, and it becomes all the more striking when one realises that the Latin term *signum* can stand for 'language symbol' as well as 'standard'. The recapturing of Latin as a language does not refer to the recovery of concrete facts; it is symbolic of the whole entity. With the recovery of pure Latin everything else is, as it were, recaptured at once.

This keen interest in language and in the possibilities of language is one of the most important aspects of humanism. So important, that it has been considered *the* essential

Orpheus, by Nicoletta da Modena, born about 1454. Orpheus, here represented with a very post-classical violin, could charm wild animals and birds. By expressing a particular situation, the artist implies universal significance: art is necessarily a civilising influence.

characteristic of it, shared as it was by all humanists at the time. This may be something of an overstatement, but it is nevertheless indisputable that the rules of rhetoric (which, incidentally, also had their place in the Middle Ages), were extremely important and influential. We must bear in mind that they were first of all concerned with the *spoken* language. Rhetoric was the doctrine of eloquence, but this eloquence expressed much more than the word does today. Rhetoric was really the theory of art, since eloquence was nothing if not art: 'rhetoric' was a term that covered virtually everything that would today be called 'poetics', and 'eloquence' was almost the same as present-day 'literature'. This shift in writing clearly demonstrates the great prominence which the written language has since then acquired. It acquired its prominence during the fifteenth century, due, of course, to the invention of the printing press. Naturally the humanists realised the immense significance of this new form of communication (and the scope of their influence can partly be explained by it), but on the other hand they clung tenaciously to the traditional rules of rhetoric. Here too they tried to integrate what are for us incompatibles but which, for them, were not at all disparate.

For them there were no great problems about this, since the civilising effect of language had been emphasised for a very long time. One of the symbolic expressions of this view is to be found in the mythical figure of Orpheus. The divine singer not only managed to tame the ferocious animals with his words, he was also known as the founder of cities and in particular as the one who had led the human race from their

barbaric animal existence to civilisation and culture. These attributes of Orpheus had long been known but it was the humanists, and especially Cristoforo Landino, who breathed new life into them. In this way, the complex intricacies of the *docta religio* had yet another element added to them: the revealer of divine truth and wisdom was also the exemplar in his use of language. And ultimately humanist rhetoric does not confine itself to language alone, since it leads to a particular way of life and thought. It will, moreover, never be incompatible with Roman religion since the latter was also known to Orpheus, albeit in a different form.

From the beginning it was argued, by Salutati in particular, and after him by Valla and many others, that the Latin language could be reinstated without detracting from religious orthodoxy. In the face of all kinds of assaults on humanism they always maintained that it was possible to be a Christian and a follower of Cicero at the same time. Initially this claim probably applied mainly to an exact and proper use of language, so that 'christianus' and 'ciceronianus' were not at all mutually exclusive. Similar claims were made later, and then Cicero's world of ideas was also included. I shall be referring again to this attitude which seems so strange to us; for the moment it is simply necessary to point out that to the humanists interest in rhetoric and the proper use of language also led to a moral way of life. One could almost say that philology gave access to philosophy. Philosophy can then be described as being wise, i.e. leading a life of wisdom, and here we have yet another instance of humanist interest in what man can and should be.

The art of living

Since we are confronted with all kinds of nuances and personal variants among the many humanists it is almost impossible to give a general description of their philosophy of life. Here again I shall have to restrict myself to one or two examples in outline. We have seen that the fifteenth century appeared to give pride of place to human existence and its value, without in any way detracting from a deep and sincere religious belief. Once again this is apparent, for instance, in the dissertations devoted to the subject of man within the community. As far as Bruni and others were concerned, all undoubtedly influenced by Cicero, man was first and foremost a citizen. His glory was chiefly attained with the work he did on behalf of the state (i.e. the city) to which he belonged. Here humanist ethics included a form of nationalism, pride in the richness and beauty of Florence or Rome, for instance. But in Ficino's or Pico's view this form of activity was thought inferior to contemplation which was the prior requisite for the ascent to true supernatural existence. Without saying so in so many words they really rejected active life in order to keep themselves free to contemplate the radiant beauty of the eternal truths. It is quite certain that during the whole century numerous discussions on the tension between the citizen's activities and the philosopher's contemplation led to a variety of conclusions. One of the most famous of these is a work by Landino, *Disputationes Camaldulenses*, in which the advantages and the disadvantages of these two ways of life are weighed against one another. Since Landino, in this work at any rate, starts from a Platonic viewpoint, his preference for contemplation, for thinking rather than action, is clearly noticeable. Deeds die with the man who performs them. Thoughts, on the other hand, survive time and have eternal value. That these were difficult if not insoluble problems is shown by the dialogue form in which these questions were argued, so that there was no need to give a definite and clear cut answer. Other works by this author however, reveal a tendency, but no more than that, to attach greater value to the active life. In general we can say that exclusive interest in the active life was rarely represented (except, perhaps, later by Machiavelli), whereas some were exclusively concerned with the contemplative life, and most were seeking a harmonious balance between the two. And it was just because of Lorenzo de' Medici's search for this balance that he received so much praise from Politian. It may also have some bearing on the fact that at more or less regular intervals Lorenzo withdrew to Careggi, outside Florence, to share Ficino's company. In addition to the search for a resolution of this tension, there was the task of trying to unite two elements of human life on earth, which are allied to this tension and of equal importance in everyday life. They are generally described as *virtù* and Fortuna, but in interpreting these concepts we come up against considerable difficulties. From ancient times Fortuna was one of the rulers of the earth. This fortune, chance, the image of all that is uncertain and changeable, was a soul appointed above our globe in the universe, the soul of the sublunary world. If it is hard to describe the ancient concept

Fortuna Amoris, by Peter Vischer (1487?–1528). The figure
balanced on a sphere and directing his progress by blowing
into a sail – which he holds and turns as he wishes – was often
used in allegories about fortune, to represent the alliance between
skill and chance. Here the winged male figure is Cupid. Two
common philosophic themes, Fortune and Love, are thus combined.

of Fortuna – of such importance to the Middle Ages as well as to the Greeks and Romans – the no less ancient idea of *virtù* becomes extremely obscure when we come to the humanists. Comprising all typically masculine characteristics like fearlessness, honour and boldness, it also stands for virtue, integrity, and honesty. Different humanists will stress different aspects of this *virtù*. But it is modern writers like Stendhal and Nietzsche who have particularly overstressed the masculine element, and to such an extent that they identified it with a thoroughly amoral attitude to life. It cannot be denied that this attitude did actually prevail at the time among some rulers and army leaders, such as Machiavelli and others. It is equally true however, that there is no trace of this amoralism in the writings of the Platonic thinkers. In their writings *virtù* was obviously moving in the direction of virtue. If *virtù* for some denoted the essentially masculine qualities (and this would show in their lives rather than in their writings), for others *virtù* could only conquer Fortuna by escaping from this earth and turning to immortal life. The credit for reconciling the two extremes goes to Leon Battista Alberti, a great writer who is aware, on the one hand, of the risks or the impossibility of the purely contemplative life, but for whom, on the other hand, *virtù* is closely bound up with goodness, with a virtuous life here on earth. Man should get hold of Fortuna and deal with her as he wishes: the element of change allows itself to be moulded by human hands, provided this moulding is an expression of human endeavour and creativity.

In this respect then, there is such a thing as humanist

individualism. And there were frequent instances of this, as we know. Burckhardt, in particular, has given us a masterly and unforgettable picture of the *condottieri* leading their armies hither and thither with no concern for morals of any kind, or of rulers like the Milanese Viscontis, similarly bent on their own interests, tenaciously and without scruple. They sought after personal glory and in this some of them were aware of precedents in the ancient texts made known by the humanists. Many of the humanists courted fame, they were full of vanity and eager for personal gain. They may all have been individualists, but only in a certain sense, and this is where Burckhardt's all too neat description tends to break down. His term individualism covers many different phenomena and loses any sharp definition in the process. To him there was an ambivalence in this individualism, even, perhaps, a fundamental contrast with the Middle Ages. Any attempt to argue further along these lines is likely to end in a battle of words. We can, at least, say with confidence that humanist thought never developed a theory comparable to what has been conceived by writers with highly individualistic tendencies since the nineteenth century. This does not mean that there were no individualists in the fifteenth century; there were, but they were in a minority. The majority did not adopt this theory, nor this way of life. Nor does any of this imply that there was no trace of individualism in the Middle Ages.

Certainly one of humanism's most characteristic features remains a concern with the full development of human potential. But just as it would be wrong to take this to be an anti-religious view, it would be equally wrong to see in it the prevailing form of individualism. On the contrary, the humanists upheld the principle that this full development of the individual could only come about in conjunction and in harmony with others. It is true that this did not refer to all men and that there was no question of a universal democracy. It referred only to a select circle of like-minded people who would work together to create a new type of man. Even people like Pico and Ficino, who went a long way in their attempts to escape from all that was mundane, both moved in a circle of friends who undoubtedly considered themselves intellectual aristocrats and who shut themselves off from the world. In this sense humanist thought has aristocratic overtones. The humanists moved only in their own circle, so that their social encounters were still isolated from the world. This is why, to our modern way of thinking, their friendships have an exalted air about them in the same way as their quarrels reveal a ludicrous and petty-minded vanity. In their ties of friendship, which were to many an essential part of *virtù*, Cicero was their model, but Platonic tendencies in general would have encouraged such ties. It was cosmic love that held the spheres in equilibrium and comprised the chain leading from God down to earth. Human love, therefore, ought not to be sensual, but rather turn man from earthly sensuality to the eternally beautiful and perfect. Feminine beauty was a reflection of the beauty of divine thought, so that love would leave sensuality behind and turn its spiritual gaze upon the eternally beautiful. Love, thus divested of all sensual elements, acquired the form of deep friendship, more easily established in the relationship between one man and another. Such deep friendship was, of course, liable to develop a physical element.

Whatever the case – and here again generalising statements are scarcely sufficient – it was in such enclosed circles that the concept of *humanitas*, which was intended to be applicable to the whole of mankind, grew as a further stage in the development of ancient and medieval ideas. Cicero was again deemed by the humanists to be its originator, though in fact it was taken by him from the Stoic philosophers. During the fifteenth century it was Bruni in particular who pointed out that only those studies referring to man's existence deserved attention. And it is quite easy to determine which studies they were. We have already seen that rhetoric, by containing a philological system, was also an introduction to a philosophy of life. Now we can add that the real subject of these studies was everything that concerned language in the strictest sense, embracing literature (in the present sense of the word), philosophy, and kindred subjects which, taken together, provided the essential studies for forming man and making him complete. They provided him with his real worth, and only through them would man become what he ought to be. Not that theology no longer played its part or had lost any of its importance. Theological doctrine as such was never questioned and the Catholic faith was never under discussion among the humanists. But the wording of the doctrine was questioned, scholastic terminology was often considered out of date and barbaric, at times it was even thought that scholastic thinking had no connection with the true faith. And even without this criticism, there was always a general desire to return to the true faith. And this return was only feasible by means of the *studia humanitatis*, which would ensure that man would discover the richness of his opportunities.

Perhaps the aim of these studies is best rendered by the modern sense of the word 'culture' or general civilisation and development. I would not claim that this is a clear description, nor do I wish to imply that this was an entirely novel concept in humanism. On the contrary, it is of Graeco-Roman origin, whence it was introduced into Christian thinking. St Augustine took it up and modified it in the process. But even up to the present day this ideal has retained its curious blend of knowledge and insight, of scientific accuracy and a deeper, general understanding as characteristic of man in his fullest being. Man was supposed to be capable of doing and knowing everything. But this capacity did not necessarily have any immediate practical purpose, since it was an end in itself. To put it slightly differently, it served only as part of man's overall development.

Even allowing that this ideal form of 'culture' has survived in our era of specialisation, we still have to recognise that it has changed in many respects since the Renaissance. To begin with, it no longer has the aristocratic quality which was so important to the humanists, and again, the essential ties between this 'culture', this civilisation, and rhetoric, grammar, and language in general, would no longer find universal acceptance. What still prevails however, is the humanist view that all this is directly connected with education, and the Renaissance abounds with pedagogical writings, all purporting in one form or another to achieve this kind of cultured and complete humanity. The best-known of them is a somewhat later work by Castiglione, describing the ideal court of Urbino and the ideal courtier. This makes it clear that although the aristocratic ideal was not confined to mere intellectual superiority, nevertheless none but the nobility could aspire to such an intellect. This view was held by practically all the humanists. Furthermore it was necessary for the courtier not only to acquire all possible knowledge, but also to train himself in many kinds of sports and games, to be an experienced horseman and an able soldier, and needless to say he must cultivate the arts. But more important than any of these, he must be constantly aware of his own limitations, shun what he could not yet master, and acquire the ability to do whatever he did with superior ease. This *sprezzatura*, this graceful and seemingly effortless demeanour, was 'culture' at its most refined and courtly. It was the art of removing all artificiality. Everything one had acquired with so much effort and strain, appeared with an air of ease and elegance.

To us (being so specialised and so serious) this refinement of 'culture' seems almost to smack of dilettantism, a game for the fashionable set. Castiglione might well give this impression, but to him this game was the subtle expression of certain cultural ideals. Besides, this same *sprezzatura*, this effortless execution of tasks which required strenuous and constant study, can be noted in Michelangelo, and he cannot be described as 'society' by any means. The charge

Title page of the 1559 edition of *The Courtier*, by Baldessar Castiglione (1478–1529). Castiglione gives an idealised account of conversations at the court of Urbino. In the fourth book of *The Courtier*, Bembo delivers a discourse on divine love written in a very different tone from the preceding books, which speak of more earthly ideals. But probably Castiglione recognised no essential difference between the four books.

of dilettantism poses a much greater problem. If this is intended to mean that the courtier can do anything and knows everything but obviously less proficiently than the 'professional', then this is ample proof of our utter lack of understanding of this ideal, due to our over-specialisation. If however, we take this dilettantism to mean (according to the original sense of the word) the joy experienced by the courtier in his actions, we would certainly be nearer the truth.

A good deal, even too much, has been said in general terms about the vivacity supposedly typical of the Renaissance, and once again as distinct from the Middle Ages. The humanist's eyes are said to be focused on man and on this world, whereas man in the Middle Ages turned his eyes to the hereafter, this earth being but a vale of tears. It would be simple to show that this view of the Middle Ages is quite untenable. I am leaving that for what it is, and I will confine myself to saying that for the Renaissance too the distinction breaks down. Not that we cannot find numerous instances of great and intense enjoyment of life, but there are as many instances of nostalgia and profound melancholy. Poetry by Lorenzo de' Medici, sculptures by Michelangelo, many philosophical dissertations bear witness to a kind of melancholy pervading humanism, and also a nostalgia for eternal beauty and truth. There is no question in the fifteenth century of carefree and thoughtless pleasure. On the contrary just because human potentialities must be deployed to the utmost, everyone was well aware of his own limitations. Only then would man discover the place he could occupy in the world, and find out what his capabilities were.

IL
LIBRO DEL CORTEGIANO
DEL
CONTE BALDESSAR
CASTIGLIONE.

Nuouamente con diligenza riuisto & corretto, secondo
l'esemplare del proprio Autore.

NEC FATISCIT

VIGILATI

IN VENETIA MDLIX.

Proportion and harmony

As a precursor to the French *honnête homme* in the seventeenth century, the dandy in the nineteenth century and the present-day gentleman, the courtier developed his potentialities in the course of his daily life. In this way his life could be said to become an artistic achievement, an accomplishment that would, however, disappear with him and dissolve into nothing. In this respect it differed essentially from works of art and science, although, of course, the art of living and the life-work were both inspired by the same principle in the fifteenth century. And since we are concerned here with the essence of humanist thought, it is only these principles that are of importance to us. Any analysis of scientific and artistic achievements would be out of place and anyway excellent studies have been devoted to both subjects.

It will be obvious that these true-blue humanists, interested as they were mainly in the improvement of the mind, which they considered of primary importance to the development of the complete man, did not contribute a great deal to the growth of the natural sciences. In the discussions – which lasted for centuries – on the significance of the 'arts and sciences', the theoretical sciences were usually rated higher than the practical ones. They were considered (however incredible it may seem to us) to offer a greater degree of certainty and have a firmer foundation. This view clearly corresponded to an attitude that preferred the invisible to the visible, the eternal to the temporal, the mind to the body.

Dürer's *Melancolia I*. The pensive goddess represents the dejection
and anxiety of the 'Saturnine' temperament of the philosopher or
artist. The tools scattered around remind us that the artist is both
scholar and engineer. The child adds a neo-Platonist touch, representing
inspiration. Dürer has used contemporary beliefs as a basis upon which to
present the first modern image of the artist as a tormented genius.

If, during the later Middle Ages, attention had been drawn to the significance of observation and experimental research, the humanists paid little attention to these things. They adhered to the traditional picture of the world although they had their own interpretation of it. Copernicus was to show that the structure of the solar system was not the Aristotelian system of his contemporaries. In true humanist fashion he traced his revolutionary views back to Pythagoras. And even later on, Kepler's ideas still showed a close kinship with the harmony of the spheres. In this organic construction of the world, in which man is a microcosmos and the universe is macro-man, the cosmos must consist of qualitatively different parts. It is not until much later, at the time of Galileo and in the course of the seventeenth century, that this view is supplanted by another, according to which space is homogeneous and hence subject to quantitative examination, resulting in exact mechanical laws. Directly related to this is the fact that other branches of science too, like physics and chemistry, did not develop along more modern lines until the concept of the universe had been reinterpreted according to mechanical laws. Previously, that is during the period of humanism, chemistry showed a greater resemblance to alchemy than to a modern science. And physics was more concerned with mysterious impulses, peculiar to the objects studied, than with accurately formulated laws. The exact observation of reality was of importance only to a very few, among whom Leonardo da Vinci is often named, and it is undoubtedly true that in many flashes of his genius one can see he understood the essential value of observation.

The Ambassadors, by Holbein, 1533. The objects between the two figures recall the medieval quadrivium: astronomy, geometry, arithmetic and music. On the ground the skull, whose true form can be seen only by looking up from the bottom right, represents perspective, yet like the broken string of the lute, symbolises death and destruction in contrast to the order and harmony of learning and art.

Left Anatomical drawing by Leonardo da Vinci. *Right* Uccello's *Chalice*. Advances in the study of anatomy and geometry helped to clarify artists' ideas and techniques. In its turn, more accurate drawing of complex forms contributed to scientific advance.

On the other hand this has given rise to the inference that his supposedly anti-humanist leanings could somehow be explained as a result of this. But the humanists themselves applied such a variety of insights to so many fields of thought that da Vinci could never have been altogether opposed to them. This was the period, for instance, when jurisprudence and medicine flourished and when the latter (with anatomy) had its effect on the art of painting. And it was at this time that the mathematical laws of perspective brought about an entirely different organisation of pictorial space.

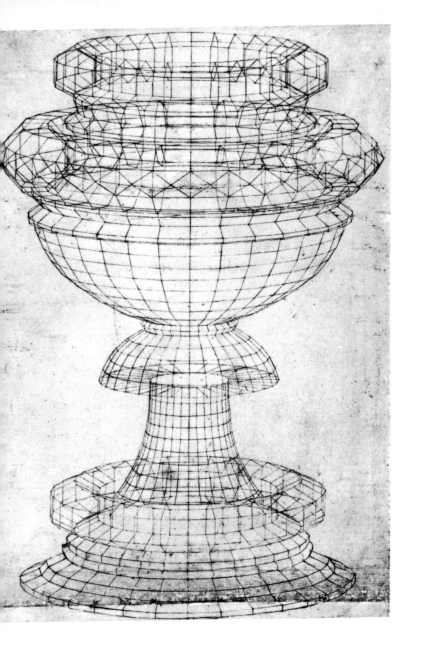

The 'divine science of perspective' made its impact in nearly every field. The word 'divine' is somewhat startling and may raise doubts about the orthodox beliefs of the humanists. But what about the many biblical pronouncements on the significance of numbers, weights and measures? Could not the whole of creation be described in those terms? And when this was taken in conjunction with the teachings of Pythagoras and cabbalistic theory, then it is understandable that the precise rules pertaining to perspective could only be called divine. They certainly caused a virtual revolution in the art of painting, where reality was now depicted as seen through a window. These rules also led to a change in the meaning and function of stage scenery, and they were of great importance to the growth of medical science, since it was henceforth possible to give a better picture of the position of the organs in relation to one another.

Directly connected with this was of course the enormous interest in proportion and harmony, almost to the exclusion of all else. This remarkable preoccupation crops up in every sphere, in the theological-philosophical observations of Nicholas of Cusa, or in Ficino's and Alberti's aesthetic treatises. These ideas are obviously applied differently in each individual case and they do not always have the same fundamental significance, but they are always there in some form. Nor is this surprising in view of the salient feature of humanist thought, their concept of harmony which expressed a mutual interrelationship between many various elements. It was pre-eminently Alberti who, following the directions left by Vitruvius, developed these ideas in architecture.

Detail from Uccello's *Battle of San Romano*,
painted about 1554–7, commemorating
Florence's victory over Siena in 1432.
Technically, this is an excellent example of
the use of perspective in painting. Note especially
the foreshortened figure in the foreground.

The harmony of a building, and hence its beauty, was created by the mutual order of the component parts attuned to one another. But, says Ficino, the same principle applies to the beauty of the human soul; here too the unity of the different parts will eventually lead to, and in any case resembles, the absolute unity which is God.

The art form in which all this, as it were, naturally converged, was for the Florentine humanists undoubtedly music.

Even if they lived for the most part among painters and sculptors (Michelangelo knew them all and in a sense he belonged to the Platonic circle round Ficino), music was nevertheless for them the art *par excellence*. Not only was music the synthesis of number and harmony, it was also the earthly rendering and the earthly example of the divine harmony of the spheres. So it is scarcely surprising that music occupied an important place in most of the occult arts. It invoked the powers, as it were, and could tune in to them; it could give expression to the forces and at the same time influence them. Thus Ficino sang Orphic hymns, musical instruments were sometimes made on the cosmic model, and according to Castiglione's precept, the courtier must have some musical understanding. In music there was a cure for melancholy, and there was an obvious relationship between the genius' divine obsession, melancholy, music and mathematical laws (demonstrated later by Dürer's *Melancolia I*); in fact the universal goal was complete and perfect harmony.

This is more easily seen in the graphic arts and in the thought of that time than in literary theories, which will for this reason be discussed later on. It was predominantly in visual imagery that the idea of roundness appealed to the sense of perfected harmony. The straight line was generally rejected and replaced by the circle and the sphere. On the plans of some churches it was no longer the cross that was recognisable, but the circle, with the result that during the sixteenth century (after the Council of Trent, when the Church marshalled its opposition to all that was considered Protestant and pagan) the building of round churches was condemned as pagan. The concept of the harmony of the individual parts, which had been of such paramount importance to the humanists, was by now losing some of its vitality. But during the fifteenth century, when humanism was at its acme, it not only seemed feasible, it was actually put into practice. This unification, this almost perfect unity, was the goal in Ficino's and Pico della Mirandola's

Detail of Titian's *Sacred and Profane Love*, 1512–15. One Venus
is of this world, the other ideal or 'philosophic' in the
Platonic sense. The picture is full of symbols taken from treatises
on love – they occur both in the fountain and in the details of
the landscape. Dialogues on the nature of love, deriving from
Plato's *Symposium*, were very fashionable in humanist circles.

thought, and was equally present in the pictures of Raphael
or Botticelli, the sculptures of Michelangelo or in the
sprezzatura of the courtier as the embodiment of the complete
man. And in all this it was intended to be the portrayal and
experience of the divine idea. Michelangelo was convinced
that the image was already there, in the block of marble in
front of him. All he had to do was to free it from all that
was superfluous and it would be visible to man's eyes in the
shape it had always had. Human labour and exertion would
bring out the harmony that had been in existence for
centuries, dormant within man's world.

At a time of great social and economic tensions, of fierce
and bloody fighting, and of frequent immoral and riotous
dissipation, humanist thought evolved its vision of complete
harmony and philosophic peace, in which the tensions would

harmonise with one another, as in music, and would to some extent be released in the process. In principle this was always attainable because the diversity of all opinions was essentially nothing but the faulty human expression of a fundamental unity, which was itself a given fact. It was towards this unity that man's life ought to be directed; this was the task of each individual. The citizen must vigilantly work for the preservation or restoration of unity in his city without ever losing sight of the perfect unity that could only be found in God. If it is true that the humanists placed man in the centre of their observations, then this was only in order that he might by contemplation identify himself with the essential order and harmony of the world and in particular of the eternal realm of the angels. In that way man would approach the inexpressible, absolute sphere of God where even harmony no longer prevailed since there were no separate parts to be found. Unity was perfect there, peace complete.

2 Erasmus

The high summer of humanist thought in Italy did not last long and at its strongest it was confined to a relatively small élite. The ideas that were developed obviously went their various ways, but in the process they lost a good deal of their original force and significance. Ficino's and Pico's ideas recur in many guises, but they have lost their vitality, they are glibly taken over and re-enacted without the involvement of the whole personality. Nevertheless, for foreigners Italy became the centre of the civilised world, so that when their ideas were carried beyond their own borders by Italian travellers or, for instance, by Ficino's correspondence, they found fertile soil abroad. There is then a definite spread of humanism during the last decades of the fifteenth century, and the aims of Florentine humanism were known to the few in Paris, Hungary, the Netherlands, Germany and especially in England. But all this remained incidental and might never have grown into a humanist 'movement', had it not been for an international figure, round whom humanism seemed to crystalise, and who was himself the personification of humanist thought, and still is today.

Erasmus still stands as one of the great names in history. With the exception of one single work, however, everything he wrote is virtually unknown. *Encomium moriae* ('Praise of Folly') is still read, it is true, but with no knowledge of his other works we are bound to gain the wrong impression of him. All the more so, since it is by no means certain that he himself thought this an important work. But even with some knowledge of the rest of his extensive writings, we

Holbein's most famous portrait
of Erasmus, now in the Louvre,
painted some time after 1523.

The Collège de Montaigu, where Erasmus, Loyola and Calvin all studied. Erasmus' views of its educational potential are enshrined in a later passage in the *Colloquies*: *Q*. Where do you come from? *A*. The College of Montaigu. *Q*. Ah, then you must be bowed down with learning. *A*. No, with lice. This feature of the place was noted also by Rabelais.

have no really clear picture of him, and he remains as mystifying a person as he was for his contemporaries. To some he seemed cowardly, or at any rate all too cautious, vain and hypersensitive to all forms of criticism, hypocritical and opportunist; to others he was a great and courageous champion of renewal, trying, by means of a never ending flow of writings, to reconcile faith and religion with the achievements of science, to do justice to all, and to restore or maintain unity in the Christian world. If we are to believe one group of his contemporaries, Erasmus was an atheist in disguise, yet according to others, he was too much of a coward to follow Luther along the road he himself had paved, and ultimately, to many Catholics he was emphatically an apostate, but the kind of apostate who did not express himself openly.

There are many different reasons for these divergent and even contrary views, which surrounded this great scholar then and which are still prevalent today. In the first place, terms like 'Lutheran' and 'atheist' were bandied about in those days when they did not have so clear a definition as they have today. That is why it is difficult to place someone who was unwilling to recognise such terms. He was unattached and did not want to commit himself, even though he was aware of a commitment, one which was not of this world's making. We are not helped either by the fact that Erasmus expressed himself so extensively and so frequently on all kinds of topics. He seems to have been in correspondence with just about the whole of Europe. Sometimes willingly, more often not, he became involved in all the

events of his day. And during his lifetime the whole complexion of modern European thought on religion and other matters underwent a change that shaped it for centuries. But this could not be seen at the time, at least not with any accuracy. No one could foresee that Protestantism, the movement that counted Erasmus among its pioneers and which he finally abandoned, was to make such a permanent mark. Before Luther's appearance, or rather Calvin's, no one could have anticipated that what many recognised as a critical situation within the Catholic Church demanded reforms which would lead to a radical split. At the beginning of the sixteenth century, there was a sense of emergency and in consequence people were forced to take new bearings. Erasmus was willing to meet this need, but in his own way: with the erudition of a great scholar who believed that world conflicts could be dealt with in books; in the noble conviction of the devout Christian whose salvation is in Christ

Est aŭt Morus præter
egregiam optimarum
literarum cognitiõem,
inter Britannicarum le
gum professores, præ
cipui nominis. .

Doctus q̃ est et graue et latine, id quod ab eo translati Luciani Dialogi mani festant.

ꝒECLAMATIO

Mole audire

c: Mala audira :꞉

A pte uo
cauit
decla
mati/
onem
ut in/
telligas rem exercendi
ingenij causa scriptam,
ad lusŭ, ac uoluptatē.
Porro Moriã fingit ue/
terum more, ceu deam
quãdam, suas laudes
narrantem, idcꝗ deco/
re, quod hoc stultis pe
culiare sit, seipsos ad/
mirari, decꝗ seipsis glo
riose prædicare. Ta
men hanc esse.) Hanc
δεικτικῶς accipiendŭ,
ut seipsam digito ostē
dat. Frontem expor/
us. Contra mœsti frontē cõ
orum Homericorum.) Face
rum natura, tamē ab Home/

Risus stul
torum

frontem expor re, non hilares mus. Contraheri non ringimus hor ã, et quid molestum ã, dicim. Phil:xi. frons et aliis, bonrŭ uir tristitia, hilari tatis, clementia, seueri tis index. Teren: Exper ge frontē ꝛc.

A section of the opening page of one copy of
Froben's 1515 edition of the *Praise of Folly*. This copy,
now in the Print Room in Basel, was decorated in the
margins by Holbein (and others). Here we see Folly,
in cap and bells, ascending the pulpit to deliver
her speech in praise of herself.

113

alone, but also with the flexibility required of the mediator,
thereby often creating the impression, though no more than
this, of insincerity, hesitancy and inconstancy. And when one
adds to this that Erasmus, in moving from place to place,
became personally involved in each new situation, despite
his academic leanings, and therewithal maintained a kind
of ironic contemplativeness, his personality certainly does
not become any more clearly defined, but it does gain in
fascination and importance.

Erasmus, who was born in 1469, was educated in Deventer
by the Brethren of the Common Life, a monastic order which,
unlike many others, concentrated on living out the teachings
of Catholicism. Averse to mysticism and theological theories,
they devoted themselves to the actual imitation of Christ's
life and ideas, as is shown by Thomas à Kempis' influential
work, *The Imitation of Christ*. Erasmus was highly receptive
to this ideal. In soaking up this uncomplicated doctrine,
which in fact was as pure and intense as any, he felt at one
with it. But while he was still in Deventer, the first echoes of
Italian humanism reached him, if only because of the affinities between Nicholas of Cusa's views – with which the
humanists often agreed – and those of the Brethren. But
there were personal contacts too. Rudolphus Agricola was a
fervent admirer of Petrarch; he had visited Platonist Florence
and Erasmus had met him once or twice. Perhaps we should
not overestimate this influence, but it is in any case a fact
that after a few years Erasmus acquired a great enthusiasm
for antiquity and a knowledge of the classics. This is apparent
from the letters which were sent from Steyn, the Augustinian

monastery which he had entered in 1488. At that time he was already working on the *Antibarbari*, his protest against ignorance, although the work was not published till much later. Moreover much of his Latin verse dates from that time, and he was engrossing himself in some of Lorenzo Valla's writings. In fact, like so many other monks, Erasmus was really a *littérateur*, a man whose main endeavours were towards a pure and proper use of language, which meant in those days classical Latin, rediscovered and practised by the humanists. So it is as a *littérateur* first and foremost that Erasmus moved to Paris to attend lectures there. This accounts for the extraordinary fact that he had relatively little contact there with theologians like Lefèvre d'Étaples, who had been so greatly influenced by Florentine Platonism, Italian philology and humanist religious beliefs. Later Erasmus was to keep up a chequered relationship with Lefèvre, but during his first stay in Paris theology was not his first concern. Now he seemed to be developing into a poet; he was publishing and heading for a literary career. Also during this period he was showing his mastery of refined Latin in his collections of colloquies for the use of his private pupils, since he had to earn his living by means of private tuition. They are the basis of his later work, which was so extensive and profound that it largely determined the thinking of the entire sixteenth century. But even at this early point in his career Erasmus was acquiring some measure of fame as a humanist, as an admirer, that is, of classical antiquity. At no point so far was his orthodoxy at issue and it was certainly not at variance with many current convictions. As a monk

Erasmus was decidly not a mystic, but equally certainly he gave no cause for offence by even creating the impression of being more sceptical than others, let alone by any atheistic tendencies. Moreover, we have ample reassurances on this score in the meeting which took place at Oxford in 1499 between Erasmus and John Colet, who was a major influence on Erasmus' life and ideas. Colet, perhaps even more than Thomas More, brought home to Erasmus the essential importance of Florentine thinking, the significance of classical antiquity for biblical studies, and the need for reform in the theological teaching and ethics of the Catholic Church.

In 1500 Erasmus, having left England for Paris, published the *Adages*, eight hundred and thirty-eight ancient sayings, in most cases accompanied by short personal observations. This collection continued to grow (by 1508, for instance, there were 3,260 of them, and it was not until 1533 that the work was cast in its final form!), while the attached observations developed more and more into highly personal reflections. It would be difficult to overestimate the significance of this work within sixteenth century European culture; for many writers and scholars these *Adages* were the chief source of their knowledge of classical antiquity and they rightly took it for the reference book it claimed to be. In this form, therefore, Erasmus' personal views acquired a currency hitherto unknown. Obviously the rapid development of printing had a great deal to do with this and perhaps Erasmus was the first – he was soon to be followed by Luther – to reap its benefits to such an extent. Moreover, the publication of this collection, and in particular its several

Pen drawing of Thomas More and his family, by Holbein.
It is thought that this was not a preliminary sketch
for a painting but a drawing from the painting (now lost)
which More sent to Erasmus. Most of the notes are in
More's handwriting, identifying the members of his
family. The drawing was found among Erasmus' papers.

revised editions, put a new complexion on humanist thought.
We have seen that Erasmus continued to add new proverbs,
new sayings, new observations to the already existing ones.
That the construction of the work permitted these additions
is due to the fact that there was no planned composition.
It has a kind of disorderliness which, however deliberate
and conscious it may be, certainly does not facilitate our
assessment of the work as a whole. It is just because of these
continuous additions and revisions that it is difficult to
ascertain Erasmus' views on a certain subject at a given time.
This kind of structure was ideally suited to his preference
for expressing himself sketchily and cautiously, and his
desire to say or suggest a great deal in a very few words,
leaving the rest to the reader (or sage!). Author and reader
are complementary and are mutually indispensable. It will
be obvious that Erasmus' way of writing, and indeed his
whole manner, failed to provide the assurances which many,
then as now, needed so badly, but which seemed to him to
put a considerable restriction on what he really meant.

Driven by many outward circumstances, but no doubt
also by an inner urge, Erasmus kept on the move, from Paris
to Steyn, France, and Belgium, finally settling in 1502 in
Louvain, where he at last embarked on what he considered
to be his real task: to show the value of the classics for the
study of the Bible, thereby achieving at the same time a
cleansing of the faith and of the Church. It is quite likely,
in fact, that this renewal was his primary aim. This, at any
rate, was when Erasmus started on his formidable labour of
preparing the works of many of the Church Fathers for

publication and of his edition of the New Testament and the important accompanying commentary. Even so, they form only a part of all that Erasmus was to produce during the course of his life, even though in themselves they are more than enough for a lifetime.

Instead of attempting a general outline of his life and works, it is sufficient here to refer to a number of these which provide typical examples of his own brand of humanism. One of these is the *Enchiridion militis Christiani* ('Manual of the Christian Soldier'), which was published in 1503 but did not make any great impact until a decade later. It contains the immediate residue of all that Erasmus had experienced in Oxford and it is still of primary importance to anyone wanting to get to grips with Erasmian humanism. What is remarkable about this book in the first place is that it is addressed to the devout layman, so that the faith is no longer a matter affecting only the clergy and the religious orders. It is not only everyone's right but his duty to concern himself with the faith. This view of religion was rapidly gaining ground at the time. Erasmus may have been a monk, but he was never to return to the monastery he left when he was still young. And he was to change his monk's habit without papal permission (which was later granted) for the attire of a gentleman of the world. Ficino too, although a priest, lived outside clerical circles, while Pico developed his religious doctrine as a layman. Right from the start Erasmus' *Enchiridion* presses home the point that Christ and only Christ demands the whole concentration of the believer, of every single believer. He should turn his back on the world, as Christ taught us; without any concern for riches, glory or honour, he is to lay himself open to the pervading spirit of God, so that he will be born again and thus become a true Christian. It is not the letter of the Gospel that counts, but the spirit, the skin must be pierced so as to penetrate to the core. Just as there is an internal and an external meaning of the Gospel text, so we have an inner and an outer man. For the outer man and all his attributes Erasmus has nothing but contempt. Ceremonies, for instance, externals which tend to obscure rather than reveal the true meaning of the Christian faith; they only become meaningful by virtue of the spirit in which they are performed; in themselves they are valueless. To value them for their own sake is to fall inevitably into the superstition of believing in what is flesh rather than in what is spirit, and this in Erasmus' view is a far too common error, often described by him as

Portrait of John Colet. Erasmus met Colet in Oxford in 1499, during his first visit to England, and conceived a great admiration for his learning and piety. It was Colet's influence as much as anyone else's that set Erasmus on the path of his life's work – the application of humanist scholarship to the interpretation of scripture.

'Judaism'. First and foremost then the *miles Christianus* should try and assimilate the true teachings of Christ and His spirit. He should set about this not hesitantly but wholeheartedly, surrendering his entire personality. His soul should thirst for Christ and have no other desires. Christ is his sole objective; when compared to him, all other aims fade into insignificance. Learning too is only of secondary importance, it can and should do no more than lead to a love of Christ: it is better to know less and to love more, than to have more knowledge and less love. And the true way to the true love of Christ is contained in the Gospel. Here then, for the first time, we find Erasmus' exclusive emphasis on the text of the New Testament, that is, on the words spoken once and for all. Here too the spirit is vastly superior to all that is material, but this of course implies the condemnation of the worship of relics, and such like.

You worship the bones of St Paul, and ought you not rather to worship the spirit of St Paul which lives in his writings? You worship an image of Christ, formed, perhaps misformed, in stone or wood, but surely you ought much rather to worship the image of His Spirit and that image can only be traced in the Gospel text.

That which is visible ought to lead man to worship the invisible and – here is the same idea again – to help him to deviate as little as possible from the law of the Gospel, which is a spiritual law, and not to lapse into Judaism.

The *Enchiridion* expresses ideas which meant a great deal to Erasmus and which remained his for the rest of his life. As we shall see, he often repeats and develops much of what

he has already said there. This work is clearly typical of his mode of thought and we shall examine now whether it is also characteristically humanistic. In Erasmus there is no evidence whatever of the frequently drawn distinction between religion on the one hand and humanist thought on the other. He was a deeply religious man, with strong objections to one or two ecclesiatical observances. The appeal to an individual experience of the faith is certainly humanistic, and so is the emphasis on language. The latter may seem unexpected, but the exclusive veneration of the Gospel, and hence of the words of Christ and the apostles, surely points in that direction. And if his faith is unimpeachable, his orthodoxy is scarcely less so. Erasmus may have been bold in condeming ceremonies and relics (for they were an essential element in the Catholic Church), but in this respect superstition had certainly grown rampant and had already aroused voices of protest before him. How could Erasmus have known, when he brought his keen mind to bear on the issue, that these protests would help to pave the way for Protestantism?

The one feature of humanism which is missing here is the emphasis on the importance of the literature of antiquity. This comes more and more to the fore in the works that followed (it was, of course, already present in the *Adages*), and it is best expressed in some of the *Colloquies*. But in so far as we are concerned with the association of humanist philology with religious problems, it is in the three *Prefaces*, which are nowadays published in one volume with his edition of the New Testament, that are of exceptional importance. They contain Erasmus' opinions regarding true Christianity and the true theology; they are the important sources for what he calls the *philosophia Christi*. This formula – probably first used by Agricola – immediately calls to mind the Italian humanists' main concern. But although we can find an element of this kind in Erasmus, his is a less speculative way of thinking; he is much more hesitant about making the kind of metaphysical observations that are found in Platonism and the *docta religio*; he has no wish to design a complete concept of the universe, and astrological or cabbalistic ideas have little appeal for him. Perhaps they were too exalted for his liking, too remote at any rate from the one and only objective, which was to offer a Christian philosophy of life, with Christ at its centre and man drawn into its orbit.

In order to achieve this the first requirement was that the account containing Christ's words and actions should be available to everybody. Erasmus was firmly convinced that literally everyone should read the Gospels, children, women, the ignorant, and this is where his opinion differed from the general view among Catholics of his time. What is more, for this he obviously required the provision of a text in an accurate rendering. This, of course, meant a return to the original source, which in turn meant that the Vulgate was bypassed and was by implication not necessarily inspired by God Himself. The points made by Lorenzo Valla earlier on were taken up again with all sorts of variations: Jerome was a great saint and a great scholar, but he was still only human; he may have been mistaken, he may have used the correct manuscripts erroneously or he may even have used the wrong manuscripts. And besides, this same translation had been exposed through the centuries to all kinds of changes, and as a result it was imperative to provide a new and correct edition. But in order to do this one should have a command of the three languages, Hebrew, Greek and Latin. (Erasmus himself, incidentally, was never to master Hebrew and was always dependent on the assistance of friends.) And if the faithful want to check on the editor's treatment of the text, they too should have a certain command of these languages.

Even though there may be grounds nowadays for questioning the scholarship of Erasmus' edition, he will always be remembered for the immensity of the critical task he undertook and for his contribution to the spread of the philological method introduced earlier in Italy. But more important still is undoubtedly the fact that this philology was not for him an aim in itself. This branch of learning was a means, admittedly an essential means, of bringing home the purity of Christ's doctrine. Similarly, literature and in particular literary theory (rhetoric) were indispensable for the scrutiny of texts and their meaning. To Erasmus – and not only to him – this argument was conclusive and inescapable and it cropped up again and again. Is it not remarkable, he argues, that all those who resist the spread of the true Christian doctrine, are also rejecting classical culture, literary art, and the *studia humanitatis* in general? For him the one was impossible without the other – in this he was a typical humanist – whereas for the monks, neither had any validity. They could be called barbaric.

Sixteenth-century printing house. The effects of
the invention of printing were not felt immediately.
Both writers and the public had to accustom
themselves to the rapid dissemination of ideas.
Erasmus was the first great writer to exploit the
potentialities of the new technique.

As for the monks, Erasmus attacked their way of living
and thinking, and ridiculed them in all sorts of ways. Or
rather, although he had nothing but praise for the original
monasticism as he visualised it, he utterly rejected the
degenerate form of it which he saw. In itself this was neither
bold nor new at the time, and here again Erasmus could
not conceivably have foreseen the results of his attacks.
An almost uninterrupted stream of anti-monastic and

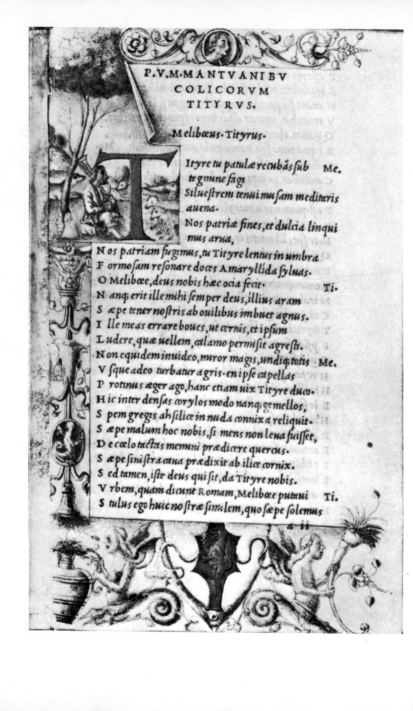

P. V. M. MANTVANI BV
COLICORVM
TITYRVS.

Melibœus. Tityrus.

Ityre tu patulæ recubás sub   Me.
te gmine fagi
Siluestrem tenui musam meditaris
auena.
Nos patriæ fines, et dulcia linqui
mus arua,

Nos patriam fugimus, tu Tityre lentus in umbra
Formosam resonare doces Amaryllida syluas.
O Melibœe, deus nobis hæc ocia fecit.   Ti.
Nanqʒ erit ille mihi semper deus, illius aram
Sæpe tener nostris ab ouilibus imbuet agnus.
Ille meas errare boues, ut cernis, et ipsum
Ludere, quæ uellem, calamo permisit agresti.
Non equidem inuideo, miror magis, undiqʒ totis   Me.
Vsque adeo turbatur agris · en ipse capellas
Protinus æger ago, hanc etiam uix Tityre duco.
Hic inter densas corylos modo nanqʒ gemellos,
Spem gregis ah silice in nuda connixa reliquit.
Sæpe malum hoc nobis, si mens non leua fuisset,
De cœlo tactas memini prædicere quercus.
Sæpe sinistra caua prædixit ab ilice cornix.
Sed tamen, iste deus quis sit, da Tityre nobis.
Vrbem, quam dicunt Romam, Melibœe putaui   Ti.
Stultus ego huic nostræ similem, quo sæpe solemus

Types used by Aldus Manutius.
Far left A page of Virgil's *Eclogues* in Aldus' revolutionary Italic type – which made feasible the printing of pocket editions. *Left* and *below* Extracts from the Lord's Prayer with a Hebrew translation, from a page of Aristotle in Aldus' large Greek type, and from a page of Bembo in the most famous of Aldus' Roman types.

qesi cælis   Pater noster
sebasamaiim   auinu
שבשמים   אבי'

nom tuü   Sáctificetur
scimcha   iithcadas
שמך.   יתקדש

regnü tuü   Adueniat
malchuthah   iauo
מלכותך.   יבא

ΑΡΙΣΟΤΕΛΟΥΣ ΑΝΑΛΥΤΙΚΩΝ ΥΣΤΕ
ΡΩΝ ΗΤΟΙ ΤΗΣ ΑΓΟΔΕΙΚΤΙΚΗΣ
ΠΡΩΤΟΝ·

Cyclops enumerat diuitias suas, haec eti
am interserit,
Est glacialis aquae riuus mihi, quem syl-
uosa
Nectareum in potum niuibus fluit Ae-
tna solutis;
aut si quae intra fagorum truncos plu-

anti-clerical literature could be traced throughout medieval Catholicism, in fact it could almost be called a very part of Catholicism itself. In these *Prefaces* therefore, Erasmus was doing no more than what had been done for centuries and what was even quite common in fifteenth-century Rome (where the close proximity of the clergy left little room for reverential treatment). To take these attacks as evidence of Erasmus' supposedly doubtful orthodoxy would be going too far. The same applies to the biting attacks on ceremonies, the cult of externals and especially scholasticism. As regards the latter his arguments run quite simply: the monks are all scholastics, scholastics lose themselves in quasi-philosophical trivialities and disputes, and what is more, all this is conducted in a horrifying kind of Latin. Monks therefore, are against the renewal of refined Latin, just as they are against the pure doctrine of Christ. They are adherents of Judaism within Christianity.

Nowadays we tend to see in these attacks an onslaught on Catholicism and the Catholic Church, for our reactions today are generally more cautious and evasive. But it would be an anachronism to transpose our views, just like that, to the beginning of the sixteenth century. At that time this kind of attack was commonplace. And it took place inside a fabric that was cracking and which was going to split (as we now know), but which, with a history of centuries behind it in which it had stood its ground against a great deal, indeed, against every onslaught, most of those who desired reform still wanted to preserve. Erasmus was certainly one of these and indeed gave proof of it. There can be no question of his showing any lack of faith; only his orthodoxy might possibly be questioned. His humanism is thoroughly Christian, and the term 'Christian humanism', which is often used to characterise his thought, is really a pleonasm.

However, we have so far been considering mainly the negative elements of the *philosophia Christi*, and when we examine the positive elements, they may well appear to be less orthodox, the more so since Erasmus here expresses himself much more circumspectly. The actual contents of this Christ-philosophy can be dealt with quite briefly. As in the *Enchiridion*, the great emphasis is once again on imitating Christ's doctrine and life. So it is right enough to call Erasmus' religion an ethical one, but quite wrong to suppose, as many do, that this kind of belief was less orthodox than the Catholicism of his time. The Gospel in Erasmus' opinion was not just for philosophical study and was not intended for the cerebral quibbles and subtle disputes which the scholastic philosophers indulged in only too readily. To Erasmus – and this is where he is a typical humanist – the Gospel was primarily a philosophy of life in that it gave the divine message telling men how to lead their lives, and what is implied by true *humanitas*. So the only concern, for the true Christian, is to live according to Christ's words. It is these words, and the meaning of them alone, that Erasmus considered important. So his thinking represents a continuation and extension in the process of spiritualising the Christian faith towards the achievement of real Christian freedom and liberation from the letter of the law. The following translation of one or two lines from the end of the first Preface (the *Paraclesis*) will provide a clear example of this, and it will also show how the extraordinary spiritual presence of Christ in his words appealed to him as a humanist.

If someone should show us traces of Christ's footsteps, we, as Christians, would worship them. How much more then should we worship His living and breathing image in His books? Out of our love of Christ we adorn His wooden or stone image with gold and precious stones. Ought we not to preserve these valuables, and others even more precious, for His books, in which He is present more than in any image? Whereas the images express only the semblance of His body (if they show any resemblance at all), the books will give us His living spirit. It is Christ Himself who is speaking, in them he is healing, dying, rising again, and He is present to such a degree that, if we could see Him with our physical eyes, He would be less visible.

The depth of faith in this passage speaks for itself. It has a mystical quality which is even more apparent in other passages where he urges 'that you may be swept away towards Christ', 'that you may be born again', 'that you may become utterly changed'.

What is remarkable here (to us at any rate), is that this mystical 'ecstasy' blends and coalesces, as it were, with a cool, critical reflection on the meaning of the text and the words. Indeed, it is in this unity that Erasmian humanism is to be found. And it is the same unity that caused many of his contemporaries to suspect his beliefs. Valla had already shown what great risks were attached to textual criticism of the Bible; evidence of the falsity of a certain document could shake the foundations of the worldly power of the papacy. Similarly, the correction of biblical texts might lead to different and new ideas. It is hardly surprising then that the Sorbonne, the theological faculty of the University of Paris and bulwark of Catholic orthodoxy, was extremely reluctant to follow this modernism, since it was virtually unaware of the need for innovations but all too conscious of the many dangers. And this is not all that could be said against Erasmus. With his ardent preoccupation with the faith, especially as laid down in the teaching of St Paul and the early Church Fathers, he was scarcely interested in the necessary organisation of the Church in this world. He was only very remotely concerned with the Church as an institution; he ranked St Paul much higher than St Peter.

Several conclusions can be drawn from this. To begin with, this accords with the general drift of humanist thought. The humanists were no less involved in Catholicism than all those who were considered orthodox, but they did turn their minds exclusively to the invisible Church, whereas to them (with no end of varying shades and degrees) the visible Church was a temporary and much less important phenomenon. Erasmus might indeed be called unorthodox, not because of what he said, but because of what he did not say. He rejected the cult of externals (unless this were accompanied by the necessary spiritual safeguards) and he was averse to scholasticism. On the other hand he had remarkably little to say on the papal status, on the significance of the Councils and even less on the various dogmas, not to mention most of the sacraments, which were also ignored. He strongly objected to hagiolatry and pilgrimages, and was doubtful about the worship of the Virgin Mary. And this can certainly be explained by the prevailing conditions, the pomp and circumstance surrounding many prelates, the licentious living of some of the clerics, the traffic in indulgences, ignorance and so one. But the circumstances were less impelling to Erasmus than his profound yearning for purity, and his intense and devout concern for the Word and the Gospel. So he might accept the dogmas but he would only refer to them in his observations very reluctantly, if at all. He was convinced that any discussion of religious dogma inevitably led to a fruitless debate and should be avoided for that reason. After all, the Gospel's purpose, which he passionately claimed to be his own, was *peace*. It was this *pax*, rooted in faith and love, and itself none other than faith and love, which was his ideal. So why should one get lost in theological disputes? God's truths exceeded by far what the human mind could attain. There are really no grounds for reading scepticism into this Erasmian aim and it is probably much nearer the truth to recognise it as a mark of wisdom and religious insight.

Naturally, the Sorbonne and many fellow-travellers had an entirely different view. This humanist interpretation of faith deviated so far from established traditions, which were for them an essential part of Catholicism, that it could no longer be considered orthodox. The phenomenal spread of Erasmus' ideas, his aversion to monasticism, his insistence on a more spiritual religion, his rejection or at any rate attenuation of all externals, his critical-philological activities, his lack of concern for the Church on earth, all these factors made his activities suspect. Even the authenticity and intensity of the *philosophia Christi* could not remedy this. Indeed, there were and still are doubts about his soundness and sincerity. Does he really say what he is thinking? Is he not often ambiguous? In order to answer these questions we had better ignore chronology and show that this undoubtedly alert mind, even after his great commentaries on the New Testament, after Luther's arrival on the scene and after the spread of Protestantism, remained loyal to the essential values of the *philosophia Christi*. His style may have retained a certain fluidity and elusiveness, but this is why it is so typical of the humanist attitude to life. The *Colloquies*, written originally for some of his pupils in Paris during his early years, were published in 1518 without his knowledge. After the event, Erasmus realised how important and useful this kind of collection could be. For this technique offered him the opportunity of presenting, in an entertaining and attractive manner, all kinds of ideas that he cherished. In this way the collection grew, like the *Adages*, and he continued working on it till 1533. Besides, there was another great advantage attached to the *Colloquies*, to which the writer cannot have been insensitive. Who is speaking in these conversations? Is it Erasmus? Or is it the person or persons who are holding the stage? In fact, this is extremely difficult to determine, so that the author can always point out that the opinions his characters are stating are not necessarily his own. There is no doubt at all that Erasmus derived exquisite pleasure from this 'game'. It is a feature ever present in his work (and it most certainly does not affect the *seriousness* of it), and becomes, for that matter, a characteristic of humanism from then on. Almost all aspects of Erasmus' thought are present in these dialogues. I will take only one of them, from the edition of 1522, containing a dissertation reminiscent of the Italian *docta religio*. The *Convivium religiosum* ('Religious Banquet') is yet another instance of the synthesis of pagan and Christian elements, expressed in the views of all those attending the feast. It also contains the well-known remark, still quoted to illustrate the lengths to which Erasmus is said to have gone. At a certain moment one of the guests uses the words, 'O holy Socrates, pray for us'. And to this day many people consider this to be the invocation in which Erasmus expressed his ridicule for Catholicism. One could obviously point out that it is not Erasmus but one of the guests speaking. What is more, it is not even the guest, for he says, 'I can scarcely help saying . . .' And why should this be just a cunning strategem? Why should we suspect him here, and not elsewhere? After all, this kind of wording fits perfectly into the framework of humanist thought. For decades, for centuries even, people had been accustomed to this mode of expression, it was part of the stock-in-trade of all those who were devoted to the *pax philosophica*. It is indicative neither of mockery nor, certainly, of lack of belief, and even less of scepticism. Perhaps it points to a kind of relativism, in which various religious beliefs were correlated with one another so as to form a unity. The same goes for another of the colloquies, *The Epicurean*, dated 1533, which is equally questionable at first sight. Is it not surely carrying things too far to see in true Christianity the most perfect realisation of epicureanism, which is (wrongly, incidentally) interpreted as the doctrine of sensual delight and worldly pleasure? Were it not for the unexpected parallel, we should not quarrel with the argument that true delight is only attainable for those with a pure conscience. Only true Christians can have this, and so they are perfect epicureans. Those who held this view maintained that this is not really paradoxical even if it seems to be. To our eyes the ambiguity seems even more blatant on account of the use of the Latin *voluptas*. Nowadays this word is invariably associated with sensual pleasure and this in turn is equated with sexual enjoyment. But there is no question of this in the Renaissance, nor in humanism. Ficino and others make frequent use of the term but always with reference to spiritual desire and the physical only figures remotely, if at all. I have dealt with this in some detail in order to redress some of the misconstructions sometimes put on Erasmus and his circle. It is essential details such as these and a host of others like them, which help us, even with difficulty, to gain some insight into the characteristic, ambiguous and yet sincere mode of expression of this humanism.

It is this same stubborn loyalty to the *philosophia Christi* that caused Erasmus to hesitate for so long with regard to Luther and Protestantism. It was this honesty which put him out of favour with opposite parties, even though he had followers and admirers in both: cardinals like Sadoleto and Pole and later Pope Paul IV and Thomas More, and among the Protestants, Oecolampadius the Basel reformer,

Bucer of Strasbourg and in particular Melanchthon, to mention only the most famous. For years, even during the Council of Trent, they tried to bring about a reconciliation in a truly Erasmian spirit. At the same time however, many Catholics were firmly convinced that Erasmus had gone much too far in his criticism of the Church and that he was primarily to blame for the Protestant movement. Luther, on the other hand, soon reproached him for not having gone far enough and for not stating his opinion openly. But the *Colloquies*, for instance, show that Erasmus did not go back on any of his criticisms of the Church and that he felt quite considerable sympathy for several of Luther's ideas. But motivated partly by caution, partly by a desire to mediate in a reconcilition, partly through ignorance (he simply could not read the German works by Luther and the Protestants), he kept aloof from Protestantism. The reasons he gave for this were entirely in character: his dislike of theological disputes and of Luther's complete and grandiose certainty which Erasmus rejected as being arrogant pride, though he could not help feeling some respect for it. But above all Erasmus, who was and remained a humanist, regretted the disturbance of order, peace and quiet, so essential for the true Christian life.

Bringing to bear all his suppleness of mind (which in itself contained an element of stubbornness) Erasmus endeavoured to preserve the peace, or at any rate his own tranquillity, in the midst of this violent clash of opinion. It was his policy not to commit himself to anything or anyone, but his position as a man of learning known and honoured all over Europe, did not make this easy. Initially Luther went to considerable trouble to win his support, but Erasmus carefully withdrew and inevitably ended up in the situation of having to come out in the open against Luther with his *De libero arbitrio* ('On the Freedom of the Will'). It is not practicable here to dwell on its religious significance or on the importance of Luther's reply, *De servo arbitrio* ('On the Enslavement of the Will'). Erasmus probably embarked on his dissertation unwillingly, particularly since he was much less of an expert than Luther in the scholastic processes of thought, and since, as we have seen, he had such a profound dislike of this kind of dogmatic dispute. Dislike of dogmatics, whatever their origins, dislike of radicalism, a deep desire for reconciliation and especially for peace, all these again have a prominent place in this work, and face to face now with Luther's absolute zealotry, they show more clearly than ever the humanist ideal. And it is on this account that people still tend to suspect Erasmus of half-heartedness. Luther's radical conviction and prophetic fury, his total surrender to the Faith and to God seemed evidence of a religious belief which made Erasmus' convictions look puny. Luther's intense faith, and nothing but faith, his emphasis on man's complete helplessness, seemed to rise from greater depths than Erasmus could show; they also made a deeper impact. Luther's well-known comment on Erasmus' New Testament commentaries, '*du bist nicht fromm*', ('you are not devout'), seems on the face of it to state an obvious truth. And indeed, Luther is right, from his point of view. And many would still agree with him today, if only unwittingly or subconsciously. We have become extremely susceptible to the tremendous tension, the explosive power which make Luther such an absorbing personality. In themselves these two aspects seem proof of the holy zeal of his convictions and his utter honesty. Nor would I attempt to deny this, but I do not think this means that there is no tension in Erasmus. His is of quite a different kind; it is of a different origin and it has a different end in view. I do not believe it is right to accuse Erasmus of having a low-tension faith. This charge only too clearly implies that Erasmus' belief is seen through Luther's eyes and later through Calvin's and later still through Pascal's. Theirs was not the only faith; there was another, no less profound and no less pure, which could be called the human-ist faith. Whereas Luther demands an all-or-nothing radica-lism, in which the majesty of God is everything and man is nothing, Erasmus posits man as being everything as well as nothing. It is commonly held that Erasmus and other human-ists were concerned with the significance and potentialities of man without God, as against Luther's view of God's omnipo-tence, but this is an erroneous distinction. On the contrary, Erasmus' belief in faith as the only salvation, although never entirely omitting the need for man's cooperation, is quite close to Luther's convictions. What does separate them in this point of dogma, is man's duty to do good works. In orthodox Catholic opinion, on the other hand, many humanists did not emphasise this enough. From every angle therefore, it is an unacceptable caricature and simplification of humanism to say that its doctrine set the omnipotence of

man against that of God. The humanist viewpoint found itself embroiled with Catholicism, with Luther, Zwingli, the Anabaptists and others, right in the midst of religious controversy. Erasmus persisted in his opinion that none of these various confessions of faith were primarily concerned with externals or with dogmas. He remained convinced that there was an inner unity among all religions and this could be achieved by looking for reconciliation and peace. This is why humanism moves among all parties and is present in all of them in varying degrees. It is perhaps its somewhat nebulous formulation, best described as ambiguity, that made this possible. But this ambiguity should never be taken for disloyalty or untrustworthiness (although Erasmus and the humanists have always been accused of both). It is the expression of a humanism that wants to remain flexible, that will not be fettered by rigid formulae and dogmas, that demands freedom of thought in order to find the pure faith, that is convinced that all religions are relative in the sense that they are or should be intimately related.

At the same time however, Erasmus' ambiguity, as a result no doubt of the influence of Lucian, developed something more, which can best be described as relativity in the modern sense of the word. Not that this is always expressed in so many words, but the *Praise of Folly* undoubtedly introduces something quite new in this particular respect. It had been an age-old custom to portray the world's and man's folly in one way or another, but now Folly herself takes the floor and holds forth on her own account. What is one to make of the attacks aimed at the Church, the monks, and so on and so forth? After all, it is only Folly talking and there is surely no need to take this seriously? Who knows? And certainly it is extremely difficult to answer this question, as it was earlier with regard to Erasmus' dialogues. Is the writer being serious or not? Yes, and no, that is all that can be said. It may be unsatisfactory from the point of view of those who want a definite pronouncement and it was a decidedly unsatisfactory reply during the first decades of the sixteenth century when ancient, sacred convictions were beginning to waver and people were looking for certainty. This was assuredly no time for standing aside from, let alone rising above party differences, and although Erasmian humanism percolated through everything and traces of it can be found throughout the entire culture of that century, it did not continue in its own specific form. The taut ambiguity of the *philosophia Christi*, in which parts are allotted both to Christ and man in the critical contemplation of the Word and the world, needed its own particular climate. And with all the so-called folly, so ironically reeled off by the relativising Folly, for Erasmus one thing is absolutely certain, the world's folly is taken up and finds its perfection in the words of St Paul: 'But we preach Christ crucified, unto the Jews a stumbling block, and unto the Greeks foolishness.'

3 Humanism and French literature

Humanism and evangelism

If it is true that humanist thought, by its use of allegory and symbolism but more especially by its striving for unity and peace in the midst of seemingly different systems and ideas, increasingly displays a particular form of sincere ambiguity, literature would be an excellent means of representing these thoughts. Literary work, after all, lives in a world of its own, even though it absorbs reality as such. Literature is primarily subject to its own laws which have no validity elsewhere. One of these is that the literary work should contain an element of representation or symbolism, so that it implies or signifies more than it actually says. 'There is more to it than meets the eye' seems in many respects a fair general description of the objective of literature.

There was certainly a connection between humanism and literature in Italy, although we tend to think first of the plastic arts because of the greater amount of research done in this field. In France, on the other hand, there is much more evidence of an affinity between humanism and literature and we only need to look at the literature to find out what the individual author's thought was. This however could not affect the multiplicity of interpretations that could be attached to the pronouncements of Erasmus and others. Moreover, during the sixteenth century the situation became extremely complicated and confused, and there is no doubt that it was also extremely puzzling for people of the time. Within Catholicism one can detect a strong tendency toward reform, but the reformers themselves were confronted

Nineteenth-century engraving
from a view of Paris at
the time of Henry IV.

with the Reformation. While some of them saw in Luther's writings the logical outcome of their own views, others remained inside the Church. At first the French tended to lump Luther and Erasmus together. Berquin, who translated Erasmus, even inserted passages from Luther's work into his translations. In the eyes of the Sorbonne, in any case, both were equally to be condemned, and the charge of 'Lutheranising' was brought against anyone who deviated from an orthodoxy that was becoming inevitably more and more rigid in the face of the attacks which were levelled at it and indeed endangered it. Violent reproaches and accusations were hurled from both sides, which does not make it any easier for us to find out what their ideas really were. The situation is further obscured by the fact that these religious disputes, flaring up to such heights, provided a cover for all kinds of political and social intrigue, so that rulers in Italy, Germany, France and England either repudiated or embraced Protestantism with the sole motive of increasing their power and influence. And finally there is the impact on French thought of Italian humanism, no longer derived only from Erasmus and in its Erasmian form, but now increasingly from Italy direct.

The situation can only be sketched here in a few words. Moreover, it was of course changing all the time, almost from year to year and, what is more, it was never the same for everyone at any given moment. All we can do then, is to have a brief look at humanism in the work of one or two great authors. But this is the moment to make it quite clear that we can scarcely discuss humanism as such. The opinions are so varied and so subtly shaded that we can really only call them identical by ignoring the differences! The differences may be more obvious on a literary analysis than on a philosophical one, but the discrepancies in their humanist views are all the more significant since they derive from the same phenomena.

As we have seen, one of the sources is Italian humanism. It has been said that its spread in France was a result of the first wars against Italy at the end of the fifteenth century, after which the French victors imported the culture of the

Lefèvre d'Étaples, scholar and theologian, who influenced Erasmus and was later influenced by him. Some of Lefèvre's ideas approach Lutheranism but he never became a Protestant.

vanquished into their own country. There may well be a germ of truth in this view, though there is no doubt that Italian thought was already making itself felt before this in a small but influential circle of French men of learning. Gaguin, Fichet and especially Lefèvre d'Étaples are obvious names to mention. Continuing a tradition of French humanism in the Middle Ages, they were greatly interested in Ficino's and Pico della Mirandola's theories, and some of them made personal contact with these scholars. Lefèvre is particularly important, since he was even more involved than those who were his models in Italy in the scholastic method taught in Paris, but even so he too attempted to enrich and perfect it by a renewal of Aristotelianism and Platonism. He started work on the production of an edition of Aristotle, using, moreover, the methods of textual criticism he had

Bernard van Orley's tapestry of the Battle of Pavia, 1525–31. It is said that the Italian wars from the 1490s onwards (this battle took place in 1525) brought humanist and Renaissance thought to France. Although there is some truth in this, it must not be forgotten that humanist ideas were well known in Parisian academic circles during the second half of the fifteenth century.

discovered in Italy, and all his notes and commentaries show the philological method so characteristic of humanism everywhere. And for him too the outcome of this was a deepening of his faith, which came very close to an intense mystical experience. Following Ficino's example, he published the hermetic writings, Dionysius the Areopagite, medieval mystics and also Nicholas of Cusa. Undoubtedly influenced by Erasmus' edition of Valla's *Notes on the New Testament*, Lefèvre wrote commentaries on five Latin psalm translations, St Paul's epistles, and other works. His scholarship and especially his conviction of the need for a personal and pure faith, and the interplay between his ideas and those of Erasmus, all these produce a 'doctrine' reminiscent of the *philosophia Christi*. There are certainly considerable differences between the two personalities (Lefèvre led the life of an ascetic recluse, whereas Erasmus remained the evangelist in the world but not of the world; the former stressed the mystical experience, the latter emphasised the imitation of Christ in life), and despite their deep respect for each other the differences of opinion endemic in their times prevented their ever becoming friends. Yet Lefèvre's views were not irreconcilable with Erasmus', and however Lutheran he was in the intensity of his radical faith, he, like Erasmus, could or would never take the final step towards Protestantism.

During the first decades of the sixteenth century his disciple Briçonnet introduced a religious doctrine, described as *évangélisme*, once again stressing purity and simplicity. Religion should not be complicated by all kinds of theological subtleties: it should follow the Bible and especially the Gospel and the words of St Paul. Though not denying the need for human initiative and good works, particular stress is laid on divine grace and on faith. That some of the disciples, whom Lefèvre and Briçonnet gathered round them in the 'Meaux Group' went over to Protestantism, can hardly be called surprising. Farel, who was later to persuade Calvin to remain in Geneva, is a well-known example. Most of them however, maintained a position that for us has an odour of duplicity or temerity. Inside the Roman Catholic Church they were critical of much that was taking place there, they emphasised the spirituality of religion and stressed the inner experience. Luther appealed to them and they were delighted to read him often, but they did not break with Catholicism. This attitude again expressed the humanist ambiguity which, however, implied – and it bears repeating – no dishonesty or falsity. On the contrary, *évangélisme* wanted to absorb the good and the true from all sides and felt that by so doing it could be less rigid, richer and more complete.

Marguerite of Navarre

It was due to the powerful protection of Marguerite of Navarre, sister of Francis I, that this *évangélisme* avoided the growing intensity of the controversy, despite the fact that it inevitably became more and more suspect in the eyes of all parties. Even her work did not escape the Sorbonne's censure and prosecution, but the influence of her personality and her royal position made it possible for this evangelism and other movements to carry on almost unmolested. As in Germany, all kinds of different 'sects' arose in France, and Marguerite of Navarre was always to have a lasting interest in them. Later, not only Luther, but also Calvin and the *libertins spirituels* found in her, as it were, a sympathetic ear and they appealed for her protection. We shall return to this briefly later on, but because the situation was so extremely complicated and continually changing it will be useful first to recall one or two relevant historical facts.

One or two dates could be said to have an almost symbolic significance in so far as they illustrate the change of circumstances:

1534. Erasmus writes his *Ecclesiae concordia* ('Harmony of the Church'). Ignatius Loyola gathers together a group of followers, later to become the Jesuits. This denotes the beginning of what is commonly, perhaps incorrectly, called the Counter-Reformation. In many places, even on the doors of royal apartments, bills or 'placards' are posted, violently attacking the value and significance of the mass. The reaction of Francis I, and of the country as a whole, is no less vehement.

1536. Death of Erasmus and of Lefèvre d'Étaples. Calvin, unlike Luther a great organiser (though never willingly), publishes his *Institutes of the Christian Religion*.

It is clear that during the 1530s the parties were becoming more clearly defined and the conflict was becoming, as it were, much more orderly. Erasmian humanism was bound to go under in these religious battles. It was in imminent danger of being pulverised between Luther and Calvin on one side and Ignatius Loyola on the other. In a sense, these names too are symbolic, for there is no denying the fact that even these two movements, for all their opposition to a hesitant and ambiguous humanism, nevertheless adopted a good many of its ideas.

Humanism, meanwhile, had scored a great and lasting gain. Following the example of Louvain and other places the King had appointed scholars to lecture in Latin, and more important, also in Greek, Hebrew and oriental languages. This was the beginning of what was later to become the Collège de France, which from 1530 onwards, unlike the Sorbonne, was going to be much more receptive to the humanist revival, wishing to serve 'culture' by allowing free entry to all. It is no accident, incidentally, that it was given that name, which expresses a certain nationalism in the face of Italian influence. Nor was it an accident that Guillaume Budé, the greatest Greek expert of his time and the King's adviser, who had demonstrated in his important philological works that Greek studies can and must lead to a substantiation of the Catholic faith, had entirely devoted himself to the foundation of this new university. For although this new institution frequently opposed the ancient traditionalist University of Paris, this does not mean that it opposed the Catholic faith and certainly not religion in general.

Whereas the Collège de France was symbolic of the humanist scholarship of the time, religious humanism was manifested in a unique form in the work of Marguerite of Navarre. Strictly speaking this makes too sharp a distinction.

Clouet's portrait of Marguerite of Navarre, sister of
Francis I and the protector of religious humanism in
France. Her works display both earthy and mystic
emotions. As with so many of her contemporaries,
deliberate or unconscious ambiguity prevents us from
reaching the essence of her thought.

All learning contained some religion since this penetrated
everywhere, and Marguerite's literary works might be
expected to contain philosophical speculations. It is through
her efforts and those of writers and scholars in her circle that
Platonism in particular spread so rapidly in France. In her
own work, moreover, which is of outstanding importance in
every respect, she expressed her personal reactions to all
that was happening at the time. Out of her extensive writings
one or two examples can be given here and I will in the
following comments confine myself to an attempt to show
why her work is so significant.

During the last few years of her life Marguerite of Navarre
wrote a play containing only four characters, all female – a
woman of the world, that is one who stands in the midst of
life, a superstitious woman, a wise and sensible woman and
finally a shepherdess, enraptured with God's love and hence
completely out of this world. I need hardly say that it is
the last one who is by far the most favoured, in fact by saying
this I have not put it nearly strongly enough. The shepherdess'
nature is of an entirely different order from that of the other
three, all of whom have a similar nature with only slight
variations. Even the wise and sensible woman has more in
common with the two reprehensible characters than with the
shepherdess. The remarkable thing here is that the enraptured
shepherdess seems almost in a trance: she sings more than
she speaks and the audience wonders if she is out of her
mind. But it is her overflowing love for God and Christ
that makes it impossible for her to use ordinary spoken
language. She has risen above it and is far away from all that

is normally human in the everyday world. Erasmian praise of folly, which was decidedly more intellectual than this play (but not entirely free from mysticism nevertheless), is taken here to such lengths that the humanist reverence for the word and for humanity has been completely set aside. Erasmus' objective, the spirit in the word, is no longer important. Instead the word must be overcome in a mystical rapture in order to attain to the spirit. No human learning, no human endeavour will ever achieve this. What is necessary is a total surrender to the divine grace. It is not surprising therefore that Erasmus, never doubting that God's deepest secrets were inscrutable, but searching nevertheless for a true understanding of the Word, was accused by Marguerite of pride and vain curiosity. Over the years she became more and more convinced that Erasmus formed too much a part of this world and that he was too strongly attached to worldly matters and worldly activities. But she in her turn was to be accused of the same error by Calvin!

The already complicated situation is made even more difficult to understand by the fact that Marguerite of Navarre too, gives an impression of ambiguity in her work. It is extraordinary to us that in some of her poetry and drama she expresses one interpretation of love, and yet elsewhere describes it in quite different terms. Her best-known work, the *Heptameron*, contains ample evidence of this. This collection of short stories, imitating Boccaccio's *Decameron* and others, introduced this typically Renaissance prose genre to France. A small group of noblemen tell each other stories and then each one of them comments on what has been

related. This technique raises the same doubts as the humanist dialogues. It cannot possibly be maintained that Marguerite of Navarre is responsible for every opinion expressed (in literature this is never so). It must be admitted however, that the author was not blissfully unaware of attitudes to love very far removed from a mystical interpretation of it. She managed, through a mediator of course, to give an extremely spicy account of adventures and views that may seem to us *risqué* and dubious. In spite of all this however, Platonic love certainly plays the noblest part. But once again we must remember that people in those days felt and thought differently from us, and realism and mysticism were not mutually exclusive. Far from it; they not only went hand in hand, but actually embraced each other. And this was possible because none of our distinctions had yet been thought of.

Rabelais

Of the many people who were in contact with Marguerite of Navarre, the first mention must be given to François Rabelais. His work about the giants Gargantua and Pantagruel, written with tremendous animation and an abundance of words, has been described as characteristic of the Renaissance and humanism. And indeed this cycle is the epic of its time, though it is not without irony and even parody. Such a description, however, brings us no nearer to the actual meaning of his work, expressed as it was at such length. What are Rabelais' views on man and on his situation in the world? The difficulty here is that all his various works are still being interpreted and modern scholars are by no means agreed as to their meaning. It is true that they are convinced that Rabelais is one of the greatest writers – and no one can deny this – but what he says, and to what extent he is a humanist, is still an open question. And anyway, what do we mean by humanist? Could he not more accurately be called a 'Lutheran' or 'Erasmian' humanist? It will be clear by now that the term humanism by no means excludes various labels. It is quite feasible for several opinions, which are to us incompatible, to converge and coalesce at any moment. It is only when humanism is interpreted, as it used to be, as an anti-religious way of thinking (and Rabelais is regarded as a humanist), that all kinds of constructions are forced upon a work, in which the author is said, for instance, to use camouflage on some occasions and not on others, and does not dare or does not want to express his real thoughts.

Not that Rabelais, in common with his fellow-humanists, does not invite this reconstruction. If the first few volumes of the whole work are not read in order of publication (the life of Gargantua, the father, appeared in 1534, and the life of Pantagruel the son, in 1532), the reader is bound to begin with the *Prologue* which was added to *Gargantua*. In many respects these lines are revealing, for instance in the numerous references to ancient writers, and yet they remain mysterious at the same time. Obviously the reader is not being addressed personally in this *Prologue*, and yet he is conscious, somehow or other (perhaps merely on account of the fact that he is reading) that he is directly involved when Rabelais, in the course of the first few lines, dedicates his work to 'most illustrious tipplers and you highly esteemed pockmarked individuals'. This kind of breezy and good-natured jocularity may not immediately place us in the paradoxical situation of the *Praise of Folly*, but it does take us in that direction. All the more so, since what follows not only displays the customary ambiguity, but even exploits it. For after this peculiar dedication Rabelais goes on to relate how Alcibiades, in one of Plato's famous dialogues, praises his teacher Socrates:

> He is like a Silenus, like one of those small boxes which look ludicrous on the outside but which contain precious herbs.

Erasmus had already compared Christ with a Silenus and in Rabelais the comparison is equally clear. The artless fun, the gigantic adventures of his heroes, the sometimes crude and even vulgar pranks described with obvious delight – we have to go through it all before reaching the inner value. The reader has to worry at it like a dog with a bone. This, in fact, is the fairly normal and familiar pattern of allegory. An accepted medieval tradition, carried on in humanist Platonism and elsewhere, reappears here in a particular guise or, as it were, in a different key. If these books are read as such, we shall find a hidden doctrine, 'profound sacraments and awe-inspiring mysteries regarding our religion, or the political or economic situation'. But just when we think we have arrived at the correct inter-pretation, Rabelais proceeds to ridicule allegory: surely people do not believe that Homer, when writing the *Iliad* and the *Odyssey*, thought of them as allegorical tales? It is Plutarch and others who interpreted them in this way, and the Florentine humanist Politian followed their example. If the reader accepts it in Homer, why should he not do the same here? If he does not believe it, he can still do so – even though Rabelais, to quote his own words, is dictating these stories while eating and drinking. Rabelais' aim in this *Prologue* has by now been achieved, the reader has now reached the stage where he is at a loss to know what to believe and what not to believe! Is the book intended as amusement and no more than that? Or is Rabelais concerned with deeper problems? Is it not possible that it is intended to be both?

What we have found in *Gargantua* we shall find, less voluminously but no less clearly, in *Pantagruel*, which was published earlier. And it is with this ambiguity in mind that the reader will have to apply himself to the whole cycle. In this connection one of the most important and famous passages of the work is the eighth chapter of *Pantagruel*, which consists of the letter Pantagruel receives from his father during his studies in Paris. Gargantua is writing from his kingdom of Utopia, a name in itself sufficiently indicative of the fantasy interwoven in Rabelais' realism. But that is not what is important here. The whole purpose of the letter, the mere fact that here a father is writing to his son, puts this in the category of pedagogic literature, so typical of the aim of humanism to create a certain 'culture', a kind of *humanitas*. As a good father should, Gargantua very soon stresses the fact that Pantagruel is embarking on his studies in circumstances much more favourable than his own had been. Divine goodness has restored light to the humanities and he himself, known as a man of great learning, would scarcely be accepted now among the small boys in the first form. The sciences have been reinstated, a beginning has been made with the study of languages. And here follows the extremely lengthy enumeration – but he is dealing with giants after all – of all that Pantagruel will have to learn: Greek, Hebrew, Latin, Arabic; and in the medieval educational system of the 'liberal arts', geometry, arithmetic and music are all particularly important. And then, of course, there is astronomy, although predictive astrology (but only the predictive) and Raymond Lull's system can be completely omitted. Medical literature is of great importance and it is remarkable that cabbalistic literature is bracketed with this. In fact, Pantagruel is to become a veritable fount of knowledge. What is typically humanistic here is that Gargantua, a few lines further down, adds an amendment, or one might call it a refinement. For it is not just a question of learning and knowledge. By themselves these are insufficient unless accompanied by a certain attitude of mind. Wisdom, essentially an unscholarly category, will never live in a malevolent human mind. Solomon in his wisdom had said as much, and Gargantua adds the words frequently repeated as a Rabelaisian statement:

science sans conscience n'est que ruine de l'âme.

That learning is directly connected with and dependent

on the whole of human nature, is certainly a view held by Gargantua-Rabelais. Thence it is but a small step to reflections on the necessity to serve, love and fear God. There is no real knowledge without belief. This is a wise and ancient precept and the humanists, with some wishful thinking, expressed the view (and this was not completely new either) that there can be no real faith without knowledge.

The religious content and significance of this text set people thinking and still does. One could almost say that each word has been weighed again and again. For instance, is it not suspicious that Gargantua speaks of a kind of immortality given by God to men while still in this life? For they can see, he says, how they perpetuate themselves in their descendants, how the one succeeds the other, and thus it will continue until the moment of the last judgment. We cannot investigate this any further here, nor the many other passages touching on the subject of God and religion. The numerous studies on this matter indicate that Rabelais in various ways and to a varying degree expresses throughout an Erasmian-evangelical theology and faith. There are frequent instances of parodies on the monastic life, but as we have seen they were already a medieval tradition, and his concept of the divine is not orthodox in the sense the Sorbonne was to attach to it, but neither this nor anything else indicates that Rabelais was irreligious, let alone atheistic.

The last few chapters of *Gargantua*, in which the 'abbaye de Thélème' is described, have always been considered a radical example of anti-monasticism. They are said to be an expression not only of Rabelais' anti-clericalism but also of the free-thinking individualism which many find so typical of humanism. There can be no doubt that these chapters are indeed the 'poem of the Renaissance' that they are said to be, but it is extremely doubtful whether what used to be the accepted interpretation is the right one. In a war, Gargantua is victorious and makes a gift of an abbey to a monk who had fought bravely in the battle and who does not always lead a life of austerity and contemplation. He may build and equip the abbey according to his own wishes. I will omit the extensive description of the building which is in many respects an example of contemporary Renaissance architecture, and go straight to the rules of life laid down for the inhabitants. Thélème is quite obviously an anti-monastery: it is to have no walls, no bell or anything of the kind, so that services and other gatherings will be held only when desired and not at the call of the bell. There will be both men and women there, all equally comely in body and soul. Once admitted they are free to enter and leave the abbey as they please. Freedom is the keyword for everything that does or does not take place at Thélème. The name of the abbey implies as much: the Greek word *thelema* means free will, so that in these pages one can listen to the echo, transposed to a key entirely its own, of the theological discussion that had recently been held between the humanist Erasmus and Luther. But what is the extent of this freedom? The answer is simple. Freedom in Thélème is unrestricted. The residents' lives are ordered not by laws and rules but by personal decisions. They rise at will, they eat, drink, work and sleep whenever it suits them. There is only one rule, and this is always being quoted: Do as you please ('*Fay ce que vouldras*'). This clause contains a brief summary of all that the unfettered individualism of the Renaissance could imply. It seems to expose the very deep roots of the humanist ideal of freedom and the contrast between this 'monastic life' and that of the Middle Ages. It would all be very simple and clear if we were not faced with one difficulty. Just as Erasmus' famous words, 'Sancte Socrates, ora pro nobis' when removed from their context give an entirely false impression, so these words of Rabelais are always quoted incorrectly or, at any rate, incompletely. For this quotation is not the whole sentence. It is true that they are printed large, but after 'Do as you please' the sentence continues 'since free men, of a good stock and well-educated, moving in the right society, are by their nature driven instinctively to good, virtuous actions . . .' Thélème does not admit just anyone! Applicants must come from good families, and this indicates a fairly radical restriction which is yet another instance of humanist aristocracy. But it is by no means enough to be of good descent. A good and thorough education, like Pantagruel's for instance, is the second and no less obligatory condition. And there is no guarantee even then that one would always take the right road. It is only in voluntary seclusion with like-minded people that one can attain to *virtù*. It is surely not unreasonable to say that this cannot legitimately be called radical individualism. On the contrary, freedom is only for those who have acquired the right to it – a right which they, by nature *and* education, both possess and acquire. Once again we find an extraordinary paradox although it did not exist for the humanist: although dependent on God, man can, through personal surrender and above all through personal knowledge, achieve his freedom in communion with others.

Bonaventure des Périers

If Rabelais displays a paradoxical ambiguity which we find strange and can only begin to understand with difficulty, the works of other writers raise even more complicated questions. After some poems and more or less realistic stories continuing the medieval tradition, Bonaventure des Périers published in 1537 a mystifying little document entitled *Cymbalum mundi*. It contains four dialogues in allegorical form, but the allegorical treatment is so effective and has been carried to such lengths and its meaning is so obscure that one wonders if it means anything at all or makes any sense. The inescapable fact seems to be that if a writer expresses himself so enigmatically as to be incomprehensible, he does so because he lacks the courage of his convictions and has to camouflage them. And what reason would he have for this if it were not to smuggle in heterodox, even atheistic opinions? This is indeed a possibility in sixteenth-century literature. On the other hand we have evidence enough that allegory was almost second nature to medieval and humanist writers. And so in itself this method proves nothing about des Périers' atheism. But there is more than just the allegory. What, for instance, are we to make of the two characters who, driven by greed and ambition, try to filch the god Mercury's book, *the* Book? Or of the three strange philosophers whose mutual accusations of lying flare up to a murderous heat? Or of the philosopher's stone, crumbled to fragments and virtueless? Or of speaking horses and dogs, and other wonders? We seem to have more than enough evidence here of the writer's lack of faith, or at any rate of his profound scepticism. Moreover, the book itself was condemned at once by the Sorbonne, and nothing was heard of the writer after that except for fulminations against him later in the sixteenth century. Up to this day this judgment has its supporters, and their position is plausible just because the issue is surrounded by interpretive problems of great magnitude. Yet this censure is open to challenge. In des Périers' day people hurled the gravest accusations at one another at the slightest provocation, and attacks made on him since then look somewhat biased. The Sorbonne's condemnation is of course an established fact – but all things considered it was couched in the mildest of terms – that although the book did not contain deliberate errors, it was nevertheless harmful and must be burnt. And how can the author's supposed atheism be reconciled with the fact that he collaborated in the French translation of the Bible by Olivetan in 1534? He could have changed his mind in the meantime, but in that case, how can we explain Calvin's subsequent attack, not on his atheism, but on his evangelical 'nicodemism', i.e. the ambiguity of his evangelism, or Marguerite of Navarre's patronage *after* his work had been condemned? The few definite facts known from his life, as well as the evidence of his work, are much more easily and naturally explained if we accept that des Périers was defending a form of evangelism, and stating that it should remain private. During those thirty critical years, when authoritative philosophers and theologians were treating each other abominably, true faith could not be discussed, and true doctrine had to be silent. The world had become a clashing cymbal, in St Paul's words and even in des Périers' title. The divine Word had become the theologians' bone of contention and a strident clamour in the world. What was there left for man to do? In the company of a few like-minded souls he must turn his back on the world and profess his faith, and experience it in silence. And this is perhaps the uttermost paradox in humanist faith: the Word speaks in silence.

Étienne Dolet

There is not much silence about Étienne Dolet. He ended his eventful life at the stake and because of this he is often regarded as the martyr of free thinking. But was he? In many respects Dolet is the typical humanist man of learning: vain, quick to take offence, over-sensitive to criticism and quick to reproach others, full of energy, vitality and enthusiasm, especially for Latin antiquity, and with a religion that is hard to define accurately. He was frequently thrown into prison but apparently this was only rarely in connection with his religious views. These are so obscure, I submit, because of his great enthusiasm for Latin antiquity and even more for the Latin tongue. In Italy, many people looked upon the study of Latin and of language in general as the ideal schooling for a better and more virtuous life. There was no true *humanitas* without a sound knowledge of the humanities. Eloquence leads to the good life. But right from the start, and certainly towards the end of the fifteenth and the beginning of the sixteenth century this art of speech, this mastery of language, had become an end in itself. This produced a cult using rhetoric in our unfavourable sense of that word. Erasmus spoke out against this Italian trend in his dialogue *Ciceronianus* (1528). Admittedly his main argument was directed against Cicero's undisputed supremacy, to which Valla, Politian and others had objected earlier, but this dialogue and the ensuing polemics also asked the question whether it was right to cultivate Latin or any other language for its own sake. Erasmus, with his firm conviction that the classics should be studied only as an introduction to the Bible took his stand here against the religious unconcern of many Italian scholars. And it is this dialogue which Dolet attacked, in the vehement fashion peculiar to him. It is wrong, however, to assume that this exuberant admiration for antiquity and for Latin is an indication of a lack of religion. Dolet's early writings and letters certainly demonstrate the typical fluctuation and exaggeration of some of the humanists, but there is nothing to suggest that Dolet was a free-thinker. He does object to the methods of torture and persecution employed by the Inquisition but at the same time he states emphatically that he does not belong to the new sects and that he hates all these innovations. He honours and respects the centuries-old faith, even though he prefers to remain outside the pernicious religious disputes. Faced with these tragedies Dolet saw himself as a spectator, and in this his attitude was typical of many humanists. Indefatigable as a controversialist and publicist, Erasmus was involved in everything and yet desired to remain unaligned and independent. Dolet's case was similar. Being easily provoked he was for ever landing himself in the most complex situations. He would prefer to remain uncommitted, but because of his vanity, and even more his amazing productivity as a scholar and editor, he found himself involved again and again. His boundless respect for Cicero's exemplary Latin restricted him to Cicero's terminology. As a result he rejected the whole of the Christian vocabulary (the word 'Christ', for example, must be avoided), though even this does not mean that we can judge him guilty of duplicity. His mixed views may reveal a shallow or weak faith, but that is not the same as hypocrisy. They are certainly typical of the development of humanism at the time, and this is particularly true of Dolet's great philological activity which places him right at the centre of learning in his period.

Maurice Scève

Dolet spent part of his short life in Lyon, where he was in contact with many scholars and men of letters. And this is the moment to take a closer look at the latter since, unlike Dolet, they were Platonists, sharing very similar Platonic views particularly in their poetry. In the course of the sixteenth century Lyon, on the roads leading to and from Italy and always an important city, became a communication centre of considerable trade and industry and a cultural focus of Italian influence. And there was no Sorbonne! This fact is indeed often overstressed to give the impression that free-thinking (equated with humanism) was allowed free rein. But even though this is an exaggeration and although the Sorbonne had a very long arm, Lyon could rightly boast of a certain degree of independence. As a result, great publishers were drawn towards this important centre.

Since Italian ideas were more or less channelled through Lyon, it is not surprising that French literature in general shows Platonic influence. This is not the place to dwell on the spread of these ideas in France; people like Symphorien Champier, Corrozet and others made their contribution to it with their translations and editions. Most of it was achieved in Marguerite of Navarre's circle and at her instigation. More important than all this is that hermetic, cabbalistic, astrological and other elements were also introduced into France along with this Platonism, with which they were so closely associated that taken together they are indistinguishable from it.

In the meantime however, a far-reaching change had been taking place in Italy, which made itself felt in France too. While continuing to take note of Ficino's translations and commentaries or Pico's editions, people in Italy now began paying attention, possibly even greater attention, to the writings of their followers, and in particular the works of their disciples in the field of literature. This, however, had lost in philosophical depth and tension what it had gained in Platonism. In literature we find fewer and fewer metaphysical reflections on man's soul and the world, less religious contemplation and idealistic reasoning. People were content to aim less high and were satisfied with a general, rather vague Platonising atmosphere, in which the Platonic view of love was given pride of place. And even this was liable to degenerate into a sophisticated game. The many and varied manifestations of this can be found in Bembo's *Gli asolani* (1505), Castiglione's *Courtier* (1528), Leone Ebreo's *Dialogues of Love* (published posthumously in 1535) on the one hand, and on the other hand in the numerous love poems by Chariteo, Tebaldeo, and so many others. This shift of emphasis meant that all the earlier facets of Platonism were eclipsed by the one dominant theme, the ideas that human love must lead to divine love, and this at once established a link with Petrarch. This connection was already there quite naturally since Petrarch's influence on Italian humanism had been immense, though chiefly on account of his prose writings, his letters and perhaps his Latin poetry. So when Platonism became assimilated into literature, Petrarch's Italian poems took their part in its development, and this produced a synthesis of literary Platonism and Petrarchism in which the various elements can scarcely be distinguished any longer.

This certainly applies in the Platonic poetry written in Lyon. There have been many attempts to point out real differences between Platonism and Petrarchism. But in view

LION.

of the fact that all this Italian literature found its way into France almost simultaneously and, one might say, *en bloc*, it is unlikely that people then were aware of distinctions we like to make. And whatever the distinctions, there is no denying the great similarity in the use of literary imagery, which can hardly be ignored in poetry.

In Lyon, there were one or two important poets whose love poetry shows these literary influences to a remarkable degree. Maurice Scève furnishes the best-known example of this in his *Délie* (1544), a series of short poems which are extremely hard to interpret. They are Platonic, Petrarchist, as well as hermetic in both the early and modern sense of the word. They not only contain some of Hermes Trismegistus' material (through the medium of Italian humanism), they are also hermetic in the more modern sense of being esoteric and seeming to contain a secret doctrine which they want to reveal and conceal at the same time. They are couched in ambivalent terms in which the woman is and is not a woman at one and the same time, in which sensual love will be purified and can become divine love, without losing sight of the erotic personification. This is already apparent from the title *Délie*, which has always been taken as an anagram of *l'Idée*, indicating that Platonism reveals itself in love towards woman, and only there. Erotic love should seemingly be so idealised that only an abstraction remains. But not so in Scève. His poems were addressed to a real woman who, being herself a great poet, returned the compliment. In responding to his love or describing her own, Pernette du Guillet plays the same game, obeying the same rules. But it would be entirely wrong to look upon it as false or dishonest and not to be taken seriously. On the contrary, this poetic game aspires to literary and psychic heights which few would be strong enough to brave and provides a setting for refined and subtle dialectics of love. 'My waiting consists of his longing for me to be entirely his, as he will be mine.' Lines like these sound artificial and hence insincere, and they are certainly far removed from what we like to call spontaneous feeling. But this does not mean that we should deny sincerity in this sort of poetic sentiment. Besides, this is just another expression of the urge to experience everything that is of this world with the mind and soul. The ties between this poetry and aspects of humanist thought are well illustrated by an anecdote connected with

Scève, telling of his deep emotion and joy when, as a student at Avignon, he discovered the tomb of Petrarch's Laura, and it is borne out particularly by Scève's later publications like *Microcosme*, the title of which says enough.

On the other hand, since this affinity was not shared by all poets, we cannot really talk of an *école lyonnaise*. A number of stories (not all of them true perhaps) were circulating about the life of Louise Labé, another great poet of the time, and these do not reveal any Platonic love. Her poems, at any rate, expose direct and uncomplicated feelings. even spontaneous passion, and are quite unconcerned about the demands of convention and only very slightly affected by literary influences. This poetry therefore, falls almost completely outside the humanist context and has in fact, a distinctly modern ring.

The Pléiade

The poets of the Pléiade, on the other hand, did create a school. Being extremely gifted literary men, they profited by all that had been tried and achieved before, though like their Italian antecedents they claimed with some justification that what they introduced was so completely new that they could speak of a breakaway from the literature that preceded them. The work of a minor poet like Jean Lemaire des Belges, who had already assimilated Italian influences early in the sixteenth century, or the works of the famous court poet Clément Marot, translator of Virgil, Ovid, and some of the Psalms, were acknowledged by the Pléiade poets, if only subconsciously, but at the same time the former was rejected as being too insignificant and the latter was dismissed as being too elegant and superficial, and one gets the impression at times that what went on in Lyon was not of much importance to them. When they resumed the humanist development of Platonic ideas, it was in their own way.

Out of the extremely important work of these authors I shall select just a few of their ideas, considering in particular their literary views. An obvious starting point is the manifesto published by Joachim du Bellay in 1549 with the title *Défense et illustration de la langue française*, a work in every respect representative of this group and the period. What is significant in the first place is that the manifesto is written in French and calls for an enrichment and refinement of the language. From the outset humanism had made use of Latin, though there had always been a certain tension between Latin and the vernacular. Its great precursor, Dante, whose importance to the Italian humanists can scarcely be overrated, had written his masterpiece in Italian and had produced his arguments defending this course. This did not prevent Petrarch from assuming that it would be primarily his Latin poems that would achieve immortality. And the *Divine Comedy* was translated into Latin later on, while the humanists continued using Latin for the most part in their writings. This in turn resulted in a growing campaign from the advocates of the vernacular. And the social pressure exercised by the printers during the second half of the fifteenth century and, more noticeably, during the sixteenth century in France, was an added factor. In order to keep the industry going, a large number of books had to be sold in a short space of time and for that reason a large number of people had to be able to read them. That was also the aim of the Protestants who wanted their opinions to become generally known, and hence began to make use of the vernacular. And finally there were growing signs of nationalism, all working in the same direction. More and more factors strengthened the belief that the vernacular could hold its own with Latin. This was already happening in Italy and following the Italian example du Bellay pointed out that the French language could express the same values and niceties as Italian and Latin. What particularly concerns us here, however, is the literary aspect of the humanist concept of *imitatio*. Even in antiquity there existed theories regarding literary imitation. Although they receded somewhat into the background during the Middle Ages, they came into their own once more in the Renaissance as part of the general reinstatement of literary theory to its former importance. Not that any of this makes it any easier to interpret *imitatio*, especially since there is a tendency today to see originality as its antithesis and to give preference to the latter because of its creative quality. The difficulty here is that we are continually in danger of using anachronistic arguments, since the concept of originality and hence its significance simply did not exist until the eighteenth century. It is true that Politian, for instance, refused to imitate Cicero and wanted to go his own way, but this was prompted by a particular dispute with ardent Ciceronians who would not waver from the footsteps of their master. So there is no connection whatever between his argument and the modern idea of originality. It should be remembered that antiquity excelled in exemplary models for the humanist writers. These models were indeed worth imitating and great honour could be gained by showing that one could achieve this imitation. Also, since the reader has as good a knowledge of the ancients as the author, they understood one another with half a word, and imitation became a kind of homage paid to the model, which at the same time proved that the imitator was capable of something similar. For imitation was not just the outcome of a random collection of sayings, metaphors or ideas taken from the works of ancient writers. The man who wants to imitate another, says du Bellay, should more or less undergo a metamorphosis. In this connection his vocabulary is typical, with words like 'devour', 'digest', 'turn to blood and food'. So we can say that the Pléiade endeavoured to make antiquity literally their own, and they themselves became revivalists of the ancient writers.

Much nearer to us than *imitatio* was the theory of divine inspiration, which was certainly not unknown to the Pléiade. On the contrary, Ronsard and many others, particularly Pontus de Tyard, proclaimed it most emphatically and saw obsession as an essential element of art. But this was nearly always coupled with *imitatio*, and it is this combination that gives their work its particular character and makes it so illogical for us. Today we are inclined to say, either inspiration and hence originality, or imitation and hence plagiarism at worst, and in any case inferior poetic art. No sixteenth-century writer was aware of being faced with this alternative;

Portrait of
Ronsard after a
woodcut by Léonard
Gaultier (1552–1641).

to him the one was impossible without the other and would always lead to it. Incidentally, the two elements that are being combined here are of totally different origin. Imitation stems in general terms from Latin rhetoric and, one could say, from scholasticism; the theory of inspiration can be traced a very long way back to Plato. Platonism and all that followed in its wake in the course of the centuries crops up in various forms in the Pléiade poets. The same applies to the more recent French combination of Platonism and Petrarchism, which, in its turn, was to pass through various phases. Whereas, for example, du Bellay in *Olive* (the first collection of poems to consist entirely of sonnets, the accepted form for this type of love lyric) had been entirely 'Platonising' in his method, he and many others soon reacted against what they now considered a childish or

Portrait of du Bellay, also by Léonard Gaultier. Gaultier made portraits of many important contemporary figures, including royalty, statesmen, scholars and artists.

dangerous fashion. However, this was soon to change again. But what is more important is that in adopting Platonism, France accepted the complete *docta religio* that went with it, through the editions and translations of Lefèvre d'Étaples, Champier, Le Fèvre de la Boderie and others. These theories re-echo in the work of many poets and particularly in Ronsard's *Hymnes*, where mention is made of daemons, the microcosmos and macrocosmos, the theory of angels, in fact many aspects of what we have noted already in Italian humanism. This is not so much a question of philosophical re-interpretation as of poetic embellishment. An interesting point is his allusion to the Druids among the many examples of age-old theologians who were also poets, philosophers and singers, and when their turn comes they just produce the same arguments that had been used by all the others.

Extract from a poem by Joachim du Bellay, written while he was
in Rome between 1553 and 1558, and reproduced from a 1573
edition of his works. The strong national feelings of the
Pléiade poets are reflected in the theme of the poem – the poet's
longing for the beauty of the Loire and for his home at Liré –
and in the use of the vernacular rather than Latin.

Quand reuoiray-ie, helas, de mon petit uillage
  Fumer la cheminee: & en quelle saison
  Reuoiray-ie le clos de ma pauure maison,
  Qui m'est une prouince, & beaucoup d'auantag
Plus me plaist le seiour qu ont basty mes ayeux,
  Que des palais Romains le front audacieux:
  Plus que le marbre dur me plaist l'ardoise fine,
Plus mon Loyre Gaulois, que le Tybre Latin,
  Plus mon petit Lyré, que le mont Palatin,
  Et plus que l'air marin la doulceur Angeuine.

Ie me feray sçauant en la philosophie,
  En la mathematique, & medicine aussi:
  Ie me feray legiste, & d'un plus hault souci
  Apprendray les secrets de la theologie:
Du lut, & du pinceau i'esbateray ma uie,
  De l'escrime & du bal . ie discourois ainsi,

It goes without saying that allegory asserts itself too. Dorat, the teacher of the few poets who at an early age formed the group later to be called the Pléiade, had taught them the allegorical manner of reading which, as we have already seen, may have been either medieval or humanist in origin. Ronsard, in any case, later defended with some force the argument that there was a certain ritual performed in poetry. Not only was the poet a kind of god, but poetic art itself was nothing but theology at its inception – allegorical theology of course, since people could grasp the secret truths only by means of images and the like.

Similarly poetry was also closely linked with music. In fact, there was so little distinction that at that time lyrical poetry was still inseparable from its musical accompaniment. Obviously Ficino's views on Orpheus the singer-theologian and Pythagoras' theories on the harmony of the spheres played their part. Ronsard thought that this was by far the best method of imitating antiquity, and the Pléiade is said, not without reason, to have formed a society in which ancient and modern music and poetic art came together again. Influenced again by Italy, the number of these societies grew in France too, soon acquiring the name of *académies*. Some of them attempted to achieve a closer and closer harmony between music and poetry in their desire to restore the original unity that had been lost. The best-known example of this is the method employed by Jean-Antoine de Baïff, who introduced the Latin metre into his French poetry and composed the accompaniment. These and similar experiments were fairly numerous during the latter half of the sixteenth century. They were not, however, experiments to test out interesting artistic innovations on sympathetic groups, and the strains of magic, astrology and such motifs that went as far back as Ficino were not to die away again for a long time to come.

It is indeed questionable whether these experiments should be called artistic at all. In fact, for centuries music had been the common ground of art and learning, and for a long time it had actually been considered more of a science than an art. This is borne out by treatises by Augustine and Boethius, and although their influence decreased during the fifteenth and sixteenth centuries, it had by no means disappeared. At any rate, the Pléiade and the poets of the next generation did not hesitate to combine this science and all other learning with their poetry. And if we now judge the scholarly poetry of the sixteenth century as a hybrid creation, we are falling again into the error of making distinctions that were simply unthinkable during that period. Indeed, Pléiade manifestos positively requested the poet to show not only inspiration but also knowledge. We might nowadays accept this if it implied only serious study of the classics. And we can understand their interest in philology and translations, even if they were surpassed in this field by true scholars like the Estienne family and Amyot. But what about astronomy, cosmology and geology? References to these abound in poetry and, what is more, in poetry that was by no means always second-rate.

This is why it is certainly not unreasonable to place French sixteenth-century literature within the compass of humanism.

Perhaps we should avoid concentrating on any one aspect of the total phenomenon, such as *imitatio* or the glorification of man (which is not a regular or prominent feature), so as to see all the aspects as meaningful, and functioning in their own right only in so far as they result from a particular attitude and experience. Whatever the seeming confusions and contradictions manifested in the literature of the sixteenth century, they are essential to it and give it its unique structure and character.

4 Montaigne and the adventure

Discoveries

It may seem strange that up to now not a word has been said about achievements of such renown and impact as the voyages of discovery. Surely, the effective doubling – in people's minds – of the earth's surface between the end of the fifteenth century and 1600 must have been of considerable significance and of far-reaching effect. Through the enterprise first of the Portuguese and then of the Italians and later of many other nations, Europe came to hear of lands, people, customs and religions, whose existence they had never suspected. And because these facts seem so important, they have been taken to mark an essential difference between the Renaissance and the Middle Ages. The long, hazardous adventures were said to be the outcome of the enterprise and vitality of the Renaissance, whereas the Middle Ages preferred the seclusion and immobility of supernatural rest. As compared to the knowledge of God, earthly reality and the domain of the Fall would be of very little or no interest to people in the Middle Ages. A good deal can be said against this traditional distinction. Not only were the Middle Ages very stirring times; they were also a period of not inconsiderable mobility. Apart from the crusades, long and arduous pilgrimages inside Europe or to the Holy Land were the order of the day, and people undertook countless and hazardous commercial journeys. The Venetians, for instance, had trade connections far into the East. And finally there were the wandering minstrels and renegade clerics roaming the continent, some of whom

Early sixteenth-century line
engraving by A. Collaert, showing
a cosmographer in his study. Science
and seamanship go hand in hand.

created a very particular kind of poetry, entirely their own.
On the other hand it has become increasingly clear that these
voyages of discovery were not undertaken solely or even
primarily out of a desire for adventure. In fact, they were
generally due to fairly well-defined imperialistic or economic causes. What is remarkable is that these causes,

which could be called new, went hand in hand with the sort of missionary zeal that had inspired the crusades. So in this respect at any rate, there seems to be no radical difference between the two periods.

Although this is interesting in itself, what is more important to us is that the immediate results of the voyages of discovery are not clearly discernible. Sometimes, it is true, we find the discovery of America and the invention of printing bracketed as the most significant events of the period, but there is no evidence that the former had any real effect on humanist thinking; whereas there is no doubt that the humanists were aware of the significance of printing, as an almost divine invention. Moreover, the economic effect of the voyages, bringing an immense accumulation of gold and silver, was felt much sooner than their impact on people's thinking, which was not really affected until the time of the Counter-Reformation. Indeed, the slowness with which the full implications of these events were appreciated is the most puzzling thing about them; scarcely a trace of reaction can be found before 1550. And once interest in the significance of the discoveries had been aroused, it affected the humanists in a way that seems strange to us but which fits completely into the pattern of their thought. Quite simply, they took the existence of these new-born worlds and fitted them into their idealised concept of antiquity, as portrayed for example in their pastoral literature. It will be clear that this refers to their ideal of the 'golden age', the age in which man's sojourn on earth was one of happiness, innocence, ease and joy. To the humanists

the natives of Brazil or North America represented the image of the ancient world given in some of the sources. At any rate they longed for a return of the original bliss on earth. Corruption had spread everywhere in Europe and so there had to be a restoration, and in the new worlds the original state of bliss had been preserved. Montaigne provides an excellent example of such a concept. In his *Préface* – though not written before the last few decades of the sixteenth century – he mentions (with some reservations) peoples still living in the sweet freedom of the first laws of nature. In a passage on 'cannibals' which has become famous, the same idea is developed, this time even more positively – these peoples are still ruled by natural laws, hardly tainted by ours at all. Hence their pure and simple naïvety. Among them there is no commerce, no literature, no magistracy, no servitude, no poverty or riches; no agriculture, no dress, no wine. And it is then but a small step to the mention of Anacreon as an example of pastoral poetry in antiquity!

This, in my opinion, is the specifically humanist reaction to the voyages of discovery, when we might have expected to find epic poetry on the exploits of merchant adventurers.

Adventurous minds

Obviously this is not to say that the period had no real adventurers. But our knowledge of them is mostly indirect, and what we know is not necessarily always of great significance. There is, however, in a totally different field, a category of people who could quite easily be described as adventurers too, although they in their search were looking for ideas. It is inevitable that the freedom or individual initiative reflected in humanism should throw some thinkers off balance. And yet it seems that these people were quite capable of putting their eccentric, even 'wild' ideas into words, and even in such a way that they can still fascinate us. Although it is not easy to classify them, they have nevertheless this in common, that their numerous, indeed far too numerous, ideas were very contagious and were apparently contained within what could be called a closed system, so close-knit in fact that they were inclined to girate in their own plane completely divorced from reality. The cohesive tension, characteristic of humanist ambiguity, breaks down, the separate elements appear to lead a life of their own and yet they must still remain interrelated. This is one reason why these thinkers leave such an impression of confusion. Moreover they were sometimes more, sometimes less independent of traditional, orthodox or humanist trends than they thought they were; it was often their extravagant personalities (which they cultivated) by which people were fascinated, and so it is not surprising that they were acclaimed and persecuted in turn. This led to a roving life where fame and imprisonment followed one another, and where they also wandered from one doctrine to another. In this way all kinds of ideas would reach the far corners of Europe and the New World. In this 'detached category' one of the most systematic is Ochino, Vicar-General of the Capuchins, who embraced Protestantism until this failed to satisfy him, when he came into contact with groups not recognising any single doctrine but the 'free spirit' (the 'Schwärmer' of Luther's fierce condemnation, who were called 'libertins spirituels' in France). Sozzini, the founder of what was later called Socinianism, is another who comes to mind, but I shall only comment on the few whose ideas had a particular bearing on certain aspects of humanist thought and its development.

The first to be mentioned then is Charles de Bouelles (or de Bouvelles or Bovillus) who, being very much aware of the tensions inherent in humanist thinking at the turn of the century, attempted to systematise them. He was a convinced adherent of the theology described by Dionysius the Areopagite; he believed in the complete impossibility of approaching God with human words, but at the same time he set great store by man's understanding in matters of religion. He was also one of the first to write about mathematics in French, and at one stage he believed he had found a system that contained a method for explaining the entire world and man's existence in it. His best-known book appeared in 1510 with the title *Liber de sapiente* ('Book on the Wise Man'). In fact his aim, and it is a specifically humanist aim, is to strive after and possess wisdom. Ideas that seem to us quite fantastic are dealt with and worked out in a highly systematic fashion. The medieval concept of the universe and man's place in it are discussed in descriptive terms that might have come straight from Pico della Mirandola, although they are expressed with less spirit and intensity: Man is made to be the critic, judge and observer of himself and the world. If then man appears to be a completely free individual, this is only because he has been created as such. Since God has not in any way withheld wisdom from man, the wise man will become the light and splendour of the world. The human mind, initially in darkness, will then come to a clear vision. Here lies the human adventure.

If this does not perhaps seem very adventurous in the modern sense of the word, the beginning of the sixteenth century produces figures who really do answer to its present meaning. One of the most spectacular, if not the most representative, of these is Paracelsus, who was in the habit of accumulating countless theories in which virtually all the humanist ideas were freely milling around. Occult medicine, natural philosophy and metaphysical observations jostle together quite incongruously; they become completely entangled with one another and end up in an utterly confusing complexity. Perhaps this is because there is less control and less talent here than we generally find among the humanists. Almost the same can be said of Agrippa of Nettesheim (Cornelius Agrippa). This philosopher-cum-magician, perhaps rather the latter, confronts us with enigmas by combining and even unifying what we would consider to be entirely contradictory elements. In spite of, or maybe just because of this confusion, his works, with their astrological, magical, musical, generally neo-Platonic, but also Paduan and Erasmian elements, had an immense influence during the entire sixteenth century and even later. He was either (secretly!) admired or publicly despised, but traces of his ideas can be found everywhere (as, for instance, in Dürer's engraving *Melancolia I*). It is, in fact, doubtful whether his *thought* can be described at all as a systematically ordered process, not just because he links entirely unconnected ideas together with the greatest of ease, but also because he coolly contradicts himself quite regularly. Early in the sixteenth century, for instance, he wrote a massive work on occult philosophy, which was not published until twenty years later. A treatise on the vanity and worthlessness of all learning, a product of Paduan and Erasmian ideas which appeared in the interim, contained a scepticism which was being echoed still in Montaigne. What is extraordinary is that this scepticism was maintained in close conjunction with occultism, and this combination of seemingly incompatible elements can be traced to Agrippa's searching preoccupation with the Bible. According to a thought

Guillaume Postel imagined a world reborn and saw himself as the prophet of the new faith. Though deeply religious, he could never commit himself to a single revelation. His works reflect his confusion and represent the universal spirit of the Renaissance gone slightly to seed. For his readers his system was too vast to be imagined, thus causing its collapse for all but himself.

process not unusual in Erasmus and certainly not in evangelism, God to him was only apprehensible through the Word, if indeed the Word could be apprehended at all. Seen in this light, Agrippa's scepticism is by no means a sign of decay and destruction. On the contrary, it might almost be called God-fearing, in the sense that it upholds an ancient tradition that all human effort is but vanity. This meant that all such activities as cabbalistic research were rejected. But we are still left with the possibility that the Gospel could have an allegorical, a more profound and secret meaning, that could be revealed by a Platonic and occult interpretation. It goes without saying that Agrippa frequently resorted to faith and superstition, to Christian and pagan examples. But this was a natural outcome of the *docta religio* of the time, and need not necessarily point to religious doubts.

However difficult we may find it to accept this, there is no doubt about the same kind of sincerity in Guillaume Postel. Apart from his great learning, of the kind so characteristic of the humanists, he was also something of a religious prophet. After prolonged studies he joined the Jesuit order in whose missionary activities he saw great possibilities for the faith, but after a short time he was gently but firmly removed from their midst. He was a man of deep and fervent religious convictions and yet he was unable to commit himself to any single creed. He saw himself as the prophet of a renewed faith and of a complete human renewal, so that the world too would be reborn. In this sense he is literally the embodiment of the Renaissance which he experienced with his entire being. Not only was he

himself the herald of the new era, he had also met (in Venice) the prophetess, the new Eve. On the basis of these experiences he wrote his numerous works, re-echoing and elaborating all the various doctrines of his day, from cabbalism to orientalism (he was one of the most distinguished professors in oriental languages at the Collège de France), from magic to Protestantism and Schwärmerei, and so on. Postel's prophesying did not achieve much, and despite the rather forced systematisation, his writings leave an impression of confusion, although the *Introductions* to the Zohar are still very readable. In many respects he might be described as an obsessed genius, and it is not surprising that at the time he was considered mad by some and was revered by others. His thinking lacks the balance of a Pico or a Ficino. All the different elements are given free rein and are yet forced into a colossal system which, just because of its unwieldy proportions, can no longer be called systematic and which, in fact, remains unintelligible to the outsider. And so Postel too, despite his prophetic fervour, is the typical individualist, for whom the adventure of the Renaissance was a solitary and introspective journey.

Jean Bodin, with the extraordinary fantasies displayed in his work, is also a most important personality within this 'group'. Not only has he left us personal reflections on political problems – topics dear to most of the humanists (and not only to them) – but he was also a thinker who broadcast clearly unorthodox opinions towards the end of the sixteenth century. He could be, and has been counted among the *achristes*, people who show Christ in a light of scepticism. He can also be regarded as a forerunner of eighteenth-century deism which among its many forms included the opinion, held by many, that God's activities ceased the moment creation was accomplished: there was, of course, a God, but after the creation the world took its own course, independent of this divine power. Something of the kind is certainly to be found in Bodin, and his Christianity does look somewhat thin. Yet it would be going much too far to consider him an unbeliever: on the contrary! In the well-known *Heptaplomeres*, written about 1592 but not published until much later, representatives of several religions (including a 'naturalist', which is more or less a deist) discuss true religion in the familiar form of a debate. It is in a primitive religion – of the kind that would be a natural outcome of the *docta religio* – a greatly simplified form of Judaism in fact, that they look for the core of all religions. Thus Judaism, Catholicism, Lutheranism, are all different elaborations of the ten commandments. For this primitive religion there must also have been a primitive language, and this must obviously have been a much simplified form of Hebrew. This was supposed to have been Adam's 'natural' language and the only language in which one could turn to God. It would be extremely interesting, though it would lead us too far astray, to discover what Bodin's views of, for instance, magic and astrology were in this connection. He was a fierce opponent of Agrippa who he considered practised daemonic rather than pure magic, and he was in general opposed to the *docta religio*. On the other hand, he was in sympathy with certain forms of astrology, recognising its importance e.g. to medicine. He may have managed to arrange his ideas more clearly than most, but the same cannot be said of the way he co-ordinates them. It is not so much that there is ambiguity in each separate idea, but that the work as a whole is subject to many interpretations.

Among all these adventurers in the world of ideas Giordano Bruno was undoubtedly the most brilliant. Not only did he produce a particularly large number of works, he also covered the most varied ground. He is also notable for occasional sorties away from his humanist base in order to bring to it the riches of his new discoveries, though at other times he tenaciously kept to well-worn tracks. For example, he definitely broke with the medieval Aristotelian view of the universe – a very rare occurrence among the humanists – and supported Copernicus' heliocentric system. On the other hand, he continued to think of the sun, like the earth and the planets, as animate beings. We need to look further; a similar duality in other fields clearly shows that Bruno alternately upheld and, in moments of genius, demolished accepted humanist theories. The best example of the former is furnished by a well-known work *Degli heroici furori* ('On Heroic Rages') (1585), which is another exposition of neo-Platonic theories, describing the soul's ascent to God and hence its return to the original and highest unity. That all this is cast in a mythical form is obviously due to the influence of Italian humanism, but it is also a direct result of the medieval method of allegory. Although the basic essentials of humanist thought are still apparent in Bruno's work in general and in this treatise in particular, the thought itself was changing under the influence of his own and other writers' original ideas. Yet in acquiring a new complexion it had retained its recognisable features. And this very ability to change its aspect and yet remain the same is typical of humanism.

Montaigne

This mutability of man and the world was given its greatest emphasis by Montaigne. At first sight Montaigne seems the very antithesis of all these adventurers; indeed the contrast seems to be so obvious that we wonder whether his life and work offer any element of adventure at all. We tend to think of him as a philosopher sitting at his desk in the seclusion of his castle tower and meditating on the numerous subjects that arouse his interest. His early life, however, was not as quiet and unruffled as all that. Born in 1533, he received his first lessons from a German tutor and their conversation was conducted entirely in Latin. This was followed by the customary education in schools and universities still largely adhering to scholastic principles. He then joined the judiciary, residing in Paris and at court. But in spite of all this our image of Montaigne is really projected by the date 1571, when he decided to retire to the seclusion of his library in his castle near Bordeaux. Yet this was not the end of the road, for he only sought the peace of his study in order to take up the pen against the Protestants in the world outside. He returned to Paris, and after the appearance of his book in 1580 he embarked on a long journey through France, Germany, Switzerland and Italy. But he still spent much of his time in his beloved tower, even when he was made mayor of Bordeaux, and in spite of these and many other activities, his work still gives us the impression that writing was really his only occupation.

Even if his life is far from uneventful, it cannot by any stretch of the imagination be described as adventurous. In fact, its only great adventure was the appearance of the *Essais*, and they reveal a very particular view of adventure. When Montaigne set himself to write he was starting on something that many of his readers were doing already, whether as established or future humanists. He was obviously studying the classics, and commenting on what they were saying and adding here and there a personal observation, but that was all. It was, in fact, the standard procedure, the best example of which was still Erasmus' *Adages*. But as in his great predecessor, so in Montaigne the personal elements increase in volume and intensity, while the numerous quotations serve as illustrations rather than points of departure. This is already evident in the first edition of the *Essais* in two volumes; the fourth edition of 1588 shows numerous additions (mostly of a personal nature) and a completely new third volume. His observations, growing in length and individuality, have become dissertations or treatises of a rather particular kind. The *essai* is born.

The last word has still not been said on this new literary form, which introduced its own new substance. What is an *essai*? What did this title mean for Montaigne? In retrospect it is not really difficult to find earlier examples, even in

Montaigne's château near Bordeaux.
Here Montaigne retired in 1571
to write the *Essais*.

antiquity, but it should be remembered in the first place that this search for antecedents was never carried out until after Montaigne's work had been read, and furthermore this does not always explain what Montaigne himself meant. Understandably the title has been described as something new and enigmatic. This is too complex a matter to deal with fully here, and one or two remarks will have to suffice. The simplest solution is perhaps to regard Montaigne's *essai* as a try-out, a kind of personal experiment with regard to everything that was taking place. The writer is *testing* reality, life, his own personality, and hence man's place in the world. Not that he considers himself committed to the results; every day he begins afresh as it were, and seems to have forgotten all previous experiments. Nor is he at all concerned about the outcome of his undertaking; the fact that he has completed the task entirely satisfies him and it is with the greatest of ease, purely for pleasure and quite arbitrarily, that he moves from one subject to another. This often makes it extremely difficult to deduce exactly at what point Montaigne's ˙personal experiences become general observations, or to what extent the argument as a whole incorporates classical or other quotations. Montaigne notes the fact, for example, that one of his teeth has come out without causing him any pain, and this leads him almost immediately to the reflection that we are dying a little every day and therefore death is but the final jolt.

There are three important factors worth mentioning here. In the first place the *essai*, as a literary genre, is scarcely bound by rules (and in this respect it does not really belong to

Title page of the first edition of Montaigne's *Essais*, published in 1580. Montaigne brought the humanist preoccupation to its logical conclusion: whereas earlier writers relied more on theoretical arguments to discuss the place of man in the world, Montaigne tried to solve the problem by generalising from the events and thoughts of his own life.

humanist literature). The writer is entirely free and he can broach any subject on the spur of the moment. He is not bound by rhetorical conventions since these simply do not exist. Nor is there as yet a specific tone for the *essai*, though it acquired one soon after Montaigne and especially after his English followers. The *essai* then is not a logically built up argument. Nor does it confine itself to an objective account of the facts. It can really be everything and nothing at the same time and it is always possible to change it. It could scarcely be fortuitous that Montaigne continued to add to his work until he died, with the result that the final text consists of many 'layers'. And had Montaigne lived a good deal longer he would almost certainly have continued to work on the *Essais* and on them alone. In a sense this had become his life-work. And herein lies the second factor of importance. Montaigne clearly relies on what he has observed in his life. The purely theoretical argument favoured by the humanists, is now founded on direct observation. That this was necessary had already been pointed out by Leonardo da Vinci. After him in France Bernard Palissy stipulated the same condition for scientific research, and now Montaigne was applying it as a general principle.

This principle gives rise to the third important factor. To some extent the *Essais* can really be read as a diary or autobiography, for in the course of this extraordinary compilation of arguments which never arrive at a general conclusion, Montaigne is telling the story of his own life, his experiences and immediate reactions. And while he is telling us about himself, his thoughts, his emotions and his

ESSAIS
DE MESSIRE
MICHEL SEIGNEVR
DE MONTAIGNE,

CHEVALIER DE L'ORDRE
du Roy, & Gentil-homme ordinaire de sa Chambre.

LIVRE PREMIER
& second.

A BOVRDEAVS.
Par S. Millanges Imprimeur ordinaire du Roy.
M.D.LXXX.
AVEC PRIVILEGE DV ROY.

desires, he is also including man's thoughts, feelings and desires in general; each individual contains the complete form of humanity. No one can discuss the one without also expressing the other. Broadly we could say that Montaigne, in describing the individual in the world, is a typically humanist author, but when he decides to describe himself, evidently deeming any individual a suitable example, humanism takes a leap forward. He enriches it, he brings it, in my opinion, to completion.

By its nature, the *essai* does not easily lend itself to any coherent summary even of just a few of the ideas Montaigne considered important. The task looks impossible right at the start, since, as we have seen, each dissertation consisted of different parts, quite possibly belonging to different periods. A later addition can throw an entirely different light on what has been said earlier, and in the end the reader will scarcely know where he is. It is quite likely that this is just what Montaigne hoped to achieve. Far from providing his readers with certainties of any kind, his desire was rather to point out how very changeable everything is when the world of events is faced with an open and sober mind and without prejudice. We find that man and the world never remain the same since everything is governed by flux; this must surely appeal to the honest observer, who will accept it all in good conscience, without either shame or regret. Montaigne would certainly have endorsed Pico della Mirandola's view that man is a chameleon, but his reaction to this would have been very different from Pico's; in Montaigne's work there is no trace of the mystical fervour

Annotated page of Montaigne's *Essais*.
The radical alterations to the text of
each edition illustrate the very essence
of his thought: man's condition is
inevitably one of flux – there are no
certainties in the world.

liuré bataille aux ennemis à pied sec, & les y auoit desfaicts;
l'esté venu, il y gaigna contre eux encore vne bataille nauale.
Sur le subiect de vestir, le Roy de la Mexique changeoit qua-
tre fois par iour d'accoustremens, iamais ne les reiteroit, em-
ployant sa desferre à ses côtinuelles liberalitez & recompen-
ses: comme aussi iamais ny pot, ny plat, ny vtensile de sa cuisi-
ne, & de sa table ne luy estoient seruis à deux fois.

Du ieune Caton.　CHAP. XXXVII.

IE n'ay point cette erreur cómune, de iuger d'autruy
selon moy, & de rapporter la condition des autres
hómes à la mienne. ie croy aysément d'autruy beaucoup de choses, où mes forces ne peuuent attaindre. La foi-
blesse que ie sens en moy, n'altere aucunement les opinions
que ie dois auoir de la vertu & valeur de ceux qui le meritent.
Rampant au limõ de la terre, ie ne laisse pas de remerquer ius-
ques dans les nuës la hauteur d'aucunes ames heroïques. C'est
beaucoup pour moy d'auoir le iugement reglé, si les effects
ne le peuuét estre, & maintenir, au moins cette maistresse par-
tie, exempte de la corruption & debauche: C'est quelque chose d'auoir la volonté bonne, quand les iambes me faillent. Ce
siecle, auquel nous viuons, au moins pour nostre climat, est si
plõbé, que le goust mesme de la vertu en est à dire, & semble
que ce ne soit autre chose qu'vn iargon de colliege. *Virtutem*
verba putant, vt lucum ligna. Il ne se recognoit plus d'action pu-
rement vertueuse: celles qui en portét le visage, elles n'en ont
pas pourtant l'essence: car le ptofit, la gloire, la crainte, l'accou-
tumance, & autres telles causes estrangeres nous acheminent
à les produire. La iustice, la vaillance, la debonnaireté, que
nous exerçons lors, elles peuuent estre dictes telles, pour la
consideration d'autruy, & du visage qu'elles portent en public, mais chez l'ouurier ce n'est aucunement vertu: Il y a vne

that spurs man towards God. Montaigne remains in his own element; he is comfortable and at home in this state of flux and he has no desire to exchange it. Whether or not the reader agrees with him is scarcely his concern; in the very first lines of his preface he announces that he has no intention of rendering any service to his readers. In all good faith he is writing a book as a reflection of himself and of himself alone. Since, however, this individual was continually changing, it is difficult to derive any definite unity from the description. Attempts have been made to remedy this by distinguishing different phases in Montaigne's development. Periods of Stoicism, Epicureanism and scepticism have been named, and it certainly cannot be denied that these different elements predominate at different times. But that scepticism is in fact present in one form or another all the time would be even harder to deny. Scepticism must here be understood to consist of a blend of doubt and reflectiveness, occurring of course in different degrees. Again, it is the inherent fluctuation that precludes a definite or permanent judgment. But to say that a lasting judgment is impossible is not to say that it is impossible to judge at all. It is as if every pronouncement can at one and the same time refer to the subject under discussion and yet imply that the same subject may be viewed differently on the next occasion. A doctrine of life can be found in Montaigne, and it is this which makes him a true humanist.

This is, of course, not the only aspect of humanist thought to be found in the *Essais*. Another is Montaigne's great admiration for the classics and his extensive knowledge of the ancient writers. One point worth mentioning in this context is that Montaigne, like the other humanists, is acquainted with Platonism in some of its forms but that he has become indifferent to it. Not that he does not share the humanist view of Socrates as being almost divine, he does admire him and very greatly, just because he was instrumental in bringing philosophy down to earth, because he always began by talking quite naturally about quite ordinary things. The Platonic argument in dialogue form, in which the presentation of conflicting views is often more important than the outcome of the argument itself, would certainly appeal to him very much. But he is entirely out of sympathy with Plato's divine abstraction. And the imagery of the Platonic and Petrarchan poets is entirely alien to him. To his mind it is so far removed from reality as to be valueless. 'My page knows all about courting; but read him a passage from Leone Ebreo and he will have no idea of what it is all about.' That is his criticism of this literature – it bears no relation to reality.

Like every other humanist Montaigne was concerned with the pedagogic problem of imparting his own particular image of the complete man and the nature of true *humanitas*. His ethics consisted of a certain number of *mores* with which children should be familiarised. It is interesting to find that he too keeps to the aristocratic tradition, and in this respect he can be compared with Rabelais, but that is where the similarity ends. For while Rabelais requires extensive, even excessive knowledge, tempered admittedly by a trained conscience, Montaigne clearly avoids stressing knowledge and acquired learning. Like Erasmus, he scorns the traditional scholars and their aping of other people's words, their comments on commentaries and their search for causes rather than realities: '*Ils laissent les choses pour les causes*'. What is really required is that a young man should learn to form his own judgment so that he can converse intelligently on matters about which he should have some knowledge. For it is through reading, travel and civilised conversation that we can obtain a clear picture of what matters in the world and can learn how to understand it. No seclusion, no bookish learning, no so-called scientific jargon will ever achieve this. The only real authority is one's own sound judgment.

Unlike his usual practice, Montaigne does not scatter his pedagogic ideas at random throughout his writings, and nearly all of them are concentrated in one or two *essais* written for a particular purpose. This is unusual because it runs counter to the principle of the *essai*, which permits of any digression and allows the author free rein to move as far as he likes away from the accepted starting point. So it need not be significant that Montaigne makes scarcely any mention of religion in these *essais* on pedagogy, the more so since he does mention it elsewhere, notably in some very lengthy *essais*, written, in principle at any rate, with that end in view. And in any case, so much has been written by now on the subject of Montaigne's Catholicism and so many contradictory views have emerged that the picture is no longer very clear. His orthodoxy has been demonstrated with as much evidence and enthusiasm as his concealed atheism or overt scepticism. Did he take religion seriously or with a pinch of salt? His life contains more than one fact to support his acceptance of religion and even his orthodoxy. Taking only his work as evidence, however, the picture is much more complex, since he treats religion with the same inconsistency as he treats everything else. There is certainly nothing that points to intense devotion, but this of itself gives us no cause to assume (as so many do) that he was an unbeliever. Like Erasmus, Montaigne had none of Luther's or Pascal's prophetic zeal. This was simply not in his nature, but this again does not prove anything. At his father's request he translated a theological work by Raymond Sebond, whose purpose was to show that faith can also be proved by means of human understanding. To this work, which had also come to the notice of Bovillus and Agrippa, Montaigne added an *Apologie*, but following his own train of thought-associations he finally demonstrates, with the help of numerous examples, that the human mind is incapable of proving anything with certainty. The certitudes of faith are not affected by this, just because they are certain. Since Montaigne thus demonstrates the opposite of what Sebond intended, he is often regarded as a fideist. This particular view of religion had been spreading considerably, aided and abetted by Paduan ideas, and its implications were that religion existed within a framework outside which it was irrelevant.

Montaigne's references to the miraculous also produce their own crop of difficulties. He makes little mention of miracles and when he does he seems very uncertain about them, attributing them solely to man's inadequate knowledge of nature or his recourse to his imagination. But this need not mean that he rejects them completely, or even that he is sceptical about religion. The tone is undoubtedly rationalistic and was the origin of irreligion at a much later date (in the eighteenth century), but to hang the same label on the cause as on the effect would be totally unfair, particularly since he is most emphatic about his acceptance of the miracles in the Gospel. And why now assume that Montaigne is just playing safe? His thinking in this matter, as in many others, is quite certainly, I submit, traditional and even conservative. He did not hold with the Protestants' free interpretation of the Bible, and like Erasmus, he was opposed to anything that caused unrest or disturbed people's peace of mind. He accepted the faith with all his personal conviction and practised it in his own way, with the result that he neither submitted himself completely to the traditional view nor rejected it entirely. He at any rate took his stand such as it was on the principle that there could be no controversy on the subject of God's unfathomable ways. To say that Montaigne is being evasive here is putting it mildly. This is mainly due to his complexity of thought which prevents him from expressing himself uniformly, for in all his reflections he places man's variability, or rather his own, at the centre. And religion is one of man's experiences in this world of changing reality. No matter how absolute we consider religion to be (and who shall decide this, Montaigne wonders), in this life, at any rate, it is subject to the human condition, and hence to life's vicissitudes as well as its routine and customs. Perhaps this is how we should interpret the well-known pronouncement which some have felt to be an expression of profound scepticism: 'We are born Christians, just as we are born inhabitants of Périgord.' It is *also* human after all, to be this kind of Christian.

Once again, Montaigne's concern is to describe the human condition. And he has no intention of glamorising anything or anybody, or himself for that matter (though a certain amount of coquetry can scarcely be avoided in this kind of autobiographical writing). The really important element in his thought is that he places man at the centre and (*pace* Pico!) keeps him there. Man should strive neither to raise himself nor lower himself: he should remain what and who he is. Where Pico felt that man could become angelic or bestial because his potentialities were infinite, Montaigne confines himself to man as he is, to human nature and to the human situation. The last few lines of his final *essai* provide a perfect illustration of this. In complete contrast to Pico's and Ficino's Italian humanism and to the soaring ascent of Bruno's thought, Montaigne, much more in agreement with Erasmus, frankly admits his fear of this transcendent flight towards the divine; these lofty and inaccessible places do not appeal to him. The centre is where he intends to stay, where man belongs and where nature has placed him. And although man can acquire stilts and live and write grandiloquently, even on stilts he has to use his own legs. Although his throne may be the highest in the world, man still has to sit quite simply on his own rump. It follows then that the most perfect way of life is to accept the ordinary human model, with no thought of miraculous deeds or exotic pretensions. In Montaigne's view, man attains an absolute, even near-divine perfection (though he seldom uses these terms) in the loyal enjoyment of his own being.

Montaigne's wisdom resides in his desire to find and maintain the happy mean. He is indeed affected by the extremes, but he maintains his position precisely half-way between them, or in what has been called the extreme centre. It is quite wrong to ascribe this theory of the *juste milieu* to spinelessness and to deny it any tension of feeling. Even worse is the suggestion that Montaigne was guilty of a cowardly respectability. This kind of opinion only misjudges his aims entirely, ignoring the fact that it was a struggle for him to arrive at this extreme centre. It is not something which he can acquire once and for all (as the Philistine would by definition); he has to recapture it every time without relinquishing the tension that marks the extremes. In this polarity lies the tension experienced each time anew.

Here, in this *via media*, is the wisdom sought and recommended by Montaigne and which as such is also typical of the whole of humanism. For as we have seen, the humanists were not solely concerned with the accumulation of knowledge, since knowledge was only a means towards enriching and perfecting the life of each individual. Right from the beginning and during the entire sixteenth century, humanists were searching above all for a philosophy which would show the way towards wisdom, reflection and introspection, and which could never be static since it was constantly being put to the test. This is another reason why we can rightly speak of an adventure, even in Montaigne who still strikes some people as 'respectable' in his retired life. Reflecting on changeable man and the changeable world is for him, and particularly for him, something of an adventure. It is true that it is an introspective adventure, without the spectacular flare of some of the other humanists, but it is no less tense, and no less courageous.

5 Renaissance and humanism

The meaning of 'Renaissance'

In the course of the preceding account, which is obviously short and very incomplete, the words 'Renaissance' and 'humanism' have been used in close association and no attempt has been made to draw any distinction between them. In this subject – and probably in all topics of cultural history – it is probably more useful to begin with relatively vague descriptions, and by listening to writers and thinkers of the age in question gradually to arrive at a definition of the concepts. This moment has now arrived and the first question that arises is where these words, used here so frequently, originate.

They are all, surprisingly, of modern origin. The least modern is probably the word 'Renaissance', although it could be maintained that the word only received its modern meaning in 1860, when Jacob Burckhardt published his greatest work, *The Civilisation of the Renaissance in Italy*. It is true, of course, that Balzac and others, and particularly Michelet, had used the word with more or less the same meaning, but it is really through Burckhardt that the term comes to denote a particular period with its own peculiar characteristics and grows into a concept. Since Burckhardt's study was published there is scarcely a chapter of it that has not been subjected to severe and justified criticism. Nevertheless this great work remains the essential and indelible starting point of the entire modern development of Renaissance studies. It has created a Renaissance image which, no matter how inaccurate or one-sided, cannot be wiped out.

Paradoxically, the image has been demolished without itself changing very much.

The current meaning of the word 'humanism' is of the same date and originates with Georg Voigt whose study, *The Revival of Classical Antiquity or the First Century of Humanism*, appeared in 1859. The word had been used at the beginning of the nineteenth century but only in a polemic on pedagogic matters which need not concern us here. What is important is that Voigt and many others after him coupled humanism with a revival of the ancient authors. The word 'humanist' is the earliest of them all and the only one which occurs in the same form in the period concerned. Even so, its date, 1512, falls after Italian humanism had reached its peak and it has a different meaning. It belongs to a set of words that have a natural place in scholastic terminology (to which the humanists were said to be opposed), even though it meant a teacher of classical literature. *Umanista* then, is part of the vocabulary of the educational practice of the time and it does not have the meaning we attach to it today. Nevertheless, the mere function of the *umanista* could justify the view that humanism, in the beginning at any rate, technically meant the study of rhetorical expression.

It is not therefore very much help to use our current terminology as a starting point. Apparently the terms were either completely unknown at the time or they had an entirely different meaning. If, on the other hand, we look for different terms which meant what we now understand by 'Renaissance' and 'humanism' we shall straightaway have some success, for even if there is still no mention of 're-birth', there is an abundance of comparable terms. In a reference to a manuscript of Catullus, the word 'resurrection' is given great prominence. Boccaccio says that thanks to Giotto the art of painting was lifted out of obscurity and revealed to the full light. And back in the fourteenth century Villani says that the works of Cimabue and Giotto resuscitated art which had become anaemic and moribund. In his efforts to characterise Cola di Rienzo, Machiavelli later used an expression like *Roma rinata*, which is surely very close to the modern word 'Renaissance'. Later still there is the word 'reborn', in the writings of Melanchthon, and during the sixteenth century the metaphor contrasting the darkness of earlier times with the existing light became more and more fashionable. The enthusiastic explanations given by Erasmus, Rabelais and many others are well-known, and there is Vasari, who also used the word *rinascita* in his famous writings on painters and the art of painting. But this was in 1550, and anyway what did they mean by this re-birth?

It may be useful to point out first of all that words like 'revival', 'resurrection', 'renewal', which appear to us so typical of that particular age, were not at all new at the time and had been known from of old. *Renovatio* in particular was a current term with a clearly Christian meaning, and the Bible continually speaks of the new man and man reborn. Expressions like these are used by Christ and St Paul, but they also occur in Isaiah and in the *Apocalypse*, as indications of one of the first requirements of Christianity. So it is far from surprising that medieval theologians, mystics and scholars were using these words all the time.

Giotto's *Kiss of Judas*. Giotto (*c.* 1266–1337) was admired
in the Renaissance period for the 'natural' quality of his
figures. It was as if the humanist and Renaissance artists
saw nature through his eyes. His indirect influence is still
greater when we realise that until modern times Western culture
in general saw nature through the eyes of the Renaissance.

The same idea played an important part in Platonic thinking too, so the Italian humanists were certainly not setting the Tiber on fire by stressing these terms and this idea. In emphasising them they are aware of carrying on a living Christian-Platonic tradition, and they would not want it otherwise. But we have still not answered the question whether this idea signified to them what it does to us.

Enough has been said about Christianity and humanism and I shall not refer to this thorny question again. But I do not think there is any doubt about the humanists' conviction that by purifying and enriching the Church, the true, original Christian faith could be rediscovered. But did this process mean to them a resuscitation of ancient culture within the Church? In the eyes of Voigt and countless others after him, this was the characteristic element in humanism. Since, as we shall see later, this construction caused very considerable confusion, it is as well to state here and now that it certainly does not tally with the facts. In praising Giotto, Boccaccio is not for a moment concerned with a re-birth of the ancients, but only with the natural forms of Giotto's figures. In other words, what had happened in the art of painting during the dark Middle Ages could not be called *natural*. And this in turn implies that in the course of the fourteenth century and during the Renaissance the concept of 'nature' was undergoing change. A concept more vague than nature would be hard to find, and I shall not venture to define it. One thing is sure, however, and that is that during the Renaissance men's view of nature was different from their predecessors', though not necessarily better. It is also certain that they were rejecting the art of their forebears, though this does not necessarily imply a revival of the ancients. It is a fact, however, that the naturalness sought by the humanists and artists was chiefly discovered among the ancients. In the course of the fifteenth century there was a growing sensitivity to the beauty and real importance of the ancient world. People were becoming more and more convinced that they were living in a new era which was clearly distinguished from the one that preceded it and which was the first to rediscover naturalness where it had always been. Perhaps the humanists found in ancient civilisation what they were looking for, but it was not this culture that made them what they were. And they were certainly convinced that the Middle Ages (with their total ignorance of Latin, as Valla believed) had no inkling of their ancient heritage. The humanists were aware of being the first to have a certain sense, and a *modern* sense, of the periodicity of history, which might be compared with the discovery of perspective in art. They were conscious of being men who, while imitating the ancients, were yet the first to discover the true nature of man and the world. Were they right?

Humanism before the Renaissance

It is important to try and answer this question however briefly, in order to clarify what was meant by the renewal and the re-birth which the humanists thought they had brought about. And this is where we really come up against the confusion mentioned earlier. After Burckhardt and Voigt it looked for a time as if certain essential characteristics of the Renaissance and humanism had been established. Individualism, the influence of classical culture, freedom within the faith or even indifference in religious matters, a relaxation in morals or even a complete rejection of all moral principles – all this was considered to be of the essence of the fifteenth century. When all this seemed to be generally accepted, the growing scholarly interest in the Middle Ages began to make it clear that the contrasts had been drawn much too crudely, and that the distinction was less clear than had been thought or hoped. And the subsequent historiography of the Renaissance and humanism has continued to contribute to our present confusion. One of the difficulties was really known from the outset. We can scarcely conceive of humanism without Petrarch and Dante, and certainly humanist thought would have developed very differently without their vast influence in the fifteenth century. But both of them lived long before then – in the period called the Middle Ages. The answer to this dilemma was relatively simple. Dante's genius was considered so timeless that he could not be tied to any period; Petrarch could, as it were, be considered the exception that tested the rule, and he could also be looked upon as the first *modern* thinker and writer. In this way the traditional classification could be maintained for the time being. But as the years progressed, more and more exceptions and special cases were discovered: holy men like Francis of Assisi and Bonaventure had exhibited a humanism that was a later influence, and Abélard had shown his individualism; these and similar instances were cited with increasing frequency and persuasion. As a result doubts arose as to whether the Renaissance had really brought about such a breach with the immediate past as the humanists supposed. After all, was not this age with all its so-called specific characteristics just a continuation of what had also existed during the Middle Ages? And to make matters worse, the Middle Ages produced their own crop of renaissances.

Passing over what had taken place during the early Middle Ages in Ravenna, for instance, at the time of Theodoric, we find the first of these proto-renaissances at the court of Charlemagne. Towards the end of the eighth century he founded a number of schools, and to them he summoned the scholars of his empire. Of these, Alcuin became the best-known and, in respect of his humanist ideas, certainly the most important. His circle at court was a kind of *académie*, where there was a definite appreciation of the importance of ancient culture and an ambition to build a new Athens which by dint of its Christianity would far surpass the original model. As we have seen, Greek was not unknown there, and it was in fact the centre of a general revival of learning.

If this was a relatively scholastic, even 'academic' revival, it impinged also and perhaps primarily on the spheres of administration and judicial organisation. But in whatever field it emerged, ancient and Christian ideals mixed freely and easily in it, as if such a marriage posed no problems. Things were rather different in the tenth century 'renaissance', where the central figure was Gerbert d'Aurillac (later to become Pope Sylvester II), tutor to Otto III. What is clear from his correspondence is that he was embarking on a veritable hunt for ancient manuscripts. He was collecting copies of everything that was important and had them brought to him from everywhere. Moreover he considered that every cultivated person should acquire his own style and usage in imitation of the ancients. He even had the typically humanist idea that proper speech and proper writing were inseparably connected with the good life. Needless to say, these ancient models did not in the least prevent him from having completely orthodox religious convictions. If he had had to choose between the good life and proper speech learnt from the ancients, he would obviously have chosen the former, but the problem did not arise. In his time, and especially at Otto III's court, sculpture and painting were clearly adapting ancient motifs to Christian ideals. This was the beginning of a definite and remarkable trend in medieval art (and thought), in which the ancient element was divested of its own meaning and function, and yet survived in some form or other in a totally different environment.

Of these proto-renaissances, the movement which occurred in the twelfth century was the first to be given the name 'renaissance', and was also the one which acquired the greatest notoriety. Nor is there any doubt about its being the most comprehensive and far-reaching of them all. The first universities at Salerno, Bologna, Paris, Montpellier, Oxford, and many new schools bear witness to this fact. There was a noticeable revival in every field, in medicine and in law, in philosophy as well as in cosmology. Translations from Greek and Arabic were legion; Aristotle was recognised as the undisputed master, and the influence of his philosophy spread rapidly. Platonism was not unknown and there was a widespread interest in Latin. The school at Chartres, founded incidentally by one of Gerbert's pupils, became one of the most important centres. Here, succeeding generations of students, some of whom became famous scholars in their turn, set about systematising philosophy in the all-embracing sense it had at the time, without ever stating a dilemma between this and their Christian beliefs. It was the great teacher Bernard of Chartres who made the well-known comment that 'we are like dwarfs seated on the shoulders of giants, so that we can survey a larger field and have a wider view than they'. He was an advocate of rhetorical education, and he introduced an Aristotelian-Platonic concept of the universe which would influence the whole of the later Middle Ages (particularly through his pupil John of Salisbury) and would retain its validity into the fifteenth century.

What was new in the fifteenth century

Even such a cursory summary may contain enough to persuade us that the fifteenth century showed no break with preceding periods, and did not produce much that was new. All that we might call typically humanistic turns out to have long roots in the past and differs only very little from what can be found much earlier. This view has its supporters, and with all the more justification since such facts of fifteenth-century history as the voyages of discovery and the art of printing did not influence people's thinking until much later.

Nevertheless I cannot go along with this opinion. It may be that individual elements of humanism and the Renaissance figured earlier in European culture, but we are left with the question whether it is right to single out various aspects and study their historical development. If one goes to work in this way – and using the so-called historical working method one can scarcely do otherwise – one may indeed find, for a given element, a striking similarity between, say, the fifteenth and the tenth century. But in the process the total picture of humanist thought during the fifteenth, the twelfth or the eighth century is lost. In short, it does not by any means follow that a historical similarity or even identity between isolated elements entitles us to equate the two cultural complexes to which these parallel elements belong. A historical structure cannot be dismantled into so many components, which are then studied separately and then reassembled. For in this way we obviously lose sight of the interrelationship of the parts at any given moment and in a given framework. And it is precisely the organisation of these parts, which may sometimes have a long lineage, that time and again produces the originality of the whole. If the thought of the humanists is examined in this way, we find that we cannot see it in their light, as a revolutionary break with the past, for this would be to deny the evidence of isolated trends and aspects. Nor can we deny that the totality of its structure is very different from any that preceded it. To give a concrete example: there is not an aspect of Pico della Mirandola's thought that cannot be found earlier in some form or other. What is more, it is quite certain that Pico (and the other humanists) did not wish it otherwise. Nevertheless the totality of Pico's thought is original and is entirely different in tone: his thinking is different. To interpret the affinities and distinctions in this way does not make it any easier to give a description of humanism perhaps, but it does enable us to see humanism both as the result of an evolution that germinated much earlier and as a fruition quite different from what preceded it. So it is neither simply an evolution, nor a revolution. In fact we can dispense with both these terms if we consider the phenomenon as an organic structure.

Perhaps this will be seen most clearly if we take a closer look at a traditional distinction between the two periods. For on first sight there appears to be a clear distinction between the freer, truly critical thinking about man and the world of the humanists and the authoritarian, clerical system so typical of the Middle Ages. As a matter of fact this latter analysis is open to criticism, but we are not concerned with that here. What is relevant is that humanist thought is authoritarian too, even if in a different way. Therefore it would be quite wrong to make the generalising statement that humanism could dispense with authority, although even this statement would need some qualification. No doubt some of the *condottieri* recognised neither God nor law, if, that is, the legends and anecdotes about them are anything to go by. And it could perhaps be held that their conduct was retrospectively justified by Machiavelli's theories, though he was always returning to ancient models. In fact, Leonardo da Vinci was the only scholar who scarcely deferred to any authority, but in many respects he was not a humanist. He was certainly not a Florentine humanist (and it may not be pure chance that he preferred Milan to Florence). Montaigne might be called another, and yet he did recognise some kind of authority as the countless quotations clearly show. It is generally evident at any rate, that the great majority of the humanists felt the need for authority: Politian may have felt no desire to imitate Cicero but he had a deep respect for the ancients; Ficino, Pico, Erasmus, even radical innovators like Copernicus and Kepler to name only a few, were all constantly appealing to their predecessors and preferably to authoritative pronouncements from the distant past. There is therefore no question of free criticism having taken the place of authority. What was changing was the nature of authority; the previous age was now less important than the distant past, and according to the humanists there was or could be harmony and even similarity between contemporary and age-old views. So we can maintain that humanism recognised only itself and its own study as irrefutable authority if, and only if, we remember that the humanists found complete satisfaction in all kinds of sources they took very seriously, however incoherent they may have been.

It is useful in this connection to look at another concept which was central to their way of thinking and which has always been taken to be characteristic of humanism. Unlike medieval scholars the humanists focused their attentions on man. To them belongs the discovery of man and the world. Both Michelet and Burckhardt have devoted impressive pages to this subject and it is difficult not to be fascinated by their persuasive argument. Almost without being aware of it, we gain the impression that the modern view of man is derived from humanism. As for the world, apart from the voyages of discovery which have already been mentioned, it is striking that science did not make a great deal of progress during this period, and even stagnated, by comparison with the Middle Ages. But the centrality of man – that is surely a revolutionary idea? Well, rather perhaps a shift of emphasis, which brought an entirely new conception, but a conception based on data of long standing. And we should also note that this shift of emphasis took place within a context which could contain it because of the free scope it offered. In fact, man and his earthly life could move into the centre of the picture without any need of a clash with Christian thought or any of the Catholic dogmas, for as we have seen there was room for this kind of view in medieval Catholicism. But it could be argued that the humanists attached much less importance to, for instance, original sin: in Florentine thought, in Erasmus' works, hardly any mention is made of it. I raise this point deliberately since this is perhaps the clearest instance of what I mean by a new conception. In Pico's allegorical dissertations, for example, this theological problem and others like it are scarcely touched upon. Yet the existence of these problems is tacitly accepted, and also their orthodox solution. If part of a whole is not illuminated, or only dimly so, this need not imply that it does not exist. The fact alone that man does not belong to the angelic sphere though capable of attaining to it, indicates that he is to some extent a fallen being. The humanists fully accepted this fall, it never occurred to them to ignore religious truths, let alone deny them, but they were equally convinced of man's many potentialities. It is this emphasis on man's potentialities within the Christian faith that gives humanism its authentic ring. With this object in view it takes up the strands of the past and weaves a new pattern.

Humanitas

Man and the world, man poised between angel and beast, here is the ambivalence of all that is human. This was a salient theme in all sorts of guises: in humanist irony and dialogue; in Erasmus' Folly no less than in Rabelais' Panurge who reels off many foolish pieces of wisdom; and whose character comes to its fullest stature in Shakespeare's wise fools. This shows that the interrelation even more than the relatively of all that is human was foremost in their minds. The one of course flows into the other and we have already noticed this in Erasmus. On the other hand, irony is almost alien to the Florentine humanism of, say, Ficino or Pico, though yet in their Platonism they stress the inter-relationship between anything that appertains to man.

Naturally arising from this is their search for a total unity, to be restored or achieved by means that need not concern us here. Among the Florentines this unity was eventually to be attained in God as the One. Unity in earthly matters was of secondary importance to them, certainly as compared with Erasmus. Erasmus' hesitancy, his unwillingness to commit himself to definite statements is largely the result of his noble ideal to find a unity that will integrate people individually and collectively. Even in Postel, where the theory can be said to run riot, there is still this same search for a united world.

It is only in Platonic-Christian thought that this unity can be experienced in a kind of ecstasy. Elsewhere the unity has to be realised on the plane of earthly diversity. Here we find another essential trait of humanist thought: the desire for harmony. When the separate parts have been interwoven harmoniously in mutual perspective and with due regard to their natural proportions, an entity will be created with all the appearance of unity, inasmuch as this can be achieved at all in the world of man. This is where humanism and the Renaissance impinge or rather, where both are seen to be striving after the same thing, each in its own way. For if we view the Renaissance not as an era (which could only be defined with the greatest difficulty in any case), but as a revival of the arts, then the essence of humanism does indeed become portrayed in the Renaissance. Paintings by Raphael, architecture by Alberti, countless works of art at that time convey in their own media what the humanists were trying to put into words. It is one of man's attributes that with the guidance of Christian belief and the example of the ancients he can create an image of human beauty and produce the harmony to which man's life can theoretically attain.

It was inevitable that this kind of elucidation would produce an ever-increasing introspection. The humanists were interested in all that concerned man, but particularly in human nature and hence in themselves. No doubt this self-consciousness also produced those features that are traditionally associated with the Renaissance: exclusive vanity, gross immorality, ambition for fame and an immortal name. This self-awareness was certainly there, and not least among princes, military leaders, popes, and artists. The intellectuals of the time however, almost invariably issued warnings against this, and it would not be difficult to compile an anthology on this subject, using selections from the works of the Italian humanists, from Erasmus, and from the scornful utterances of Montaigne. Montaigne in particular shows this introspection in a form entirely his own. The genre of biography which, like the portrait in painting, had good reason to be popular in the Renaissance, often became autobiography in Montaigne, and until then that had been rare. And whereas the humanist biography showed strongly moralistic tendencies, so that the life described really became the exemplar to be emulated, the introspection in the *Essais* is devoted first and foremost to the self. Montaigne wants to hear his own voice, the voice of an ordinary individual imparting ordinary information rather than profound dissertations, for only thus can the private individual display humanity. A human being is the manifestation of mankind and the only possible form in which humanity can appear.

What makes man human is his *humanitas*. The word is difficult to translate because it has acquired meanings down the years that have eclipsed the peculiarly humanistic meanings. This accounts for our astonishment that *humanitas* was a concept of the fifteenth and sixteenth centuries. For this is the period of wholesale wars, bloody feuds and quarrels, the stake and the execution block, and as for tolerance, it scarcely existed even in the sixteenth century. That it existed at all was admittedly due to humanist and Erasmian ideas. But at the outset there was little in common between tolerance and this concept of *humanitas*. This was much more concerned with the complete activity of being human which must come to perfect fruition in every individual. In this way a balance between the various qualities could be developed which, in the harmoniously integrated individual, would be revealed in its finest form. But since man lived in the society of others, *humanitas* always implied a sense of community, a deep awareness of being a citizen of a town or state, with the obligation to serve it. Particularly the early Florentine historiographers like Bruni and Guicciardini (most of them were urban magistrates) rediscovered this form of *humanitas* in their Roman models as well as in the history of their own city. It is through this sense of being completely human that *humanitas* can approach *virtù*, by which man can either wrestle with Fortuna or gain the mastery over her at the opportune moment.

This 'human reaction', this living life to the full as the men we are, is not achieved naturally or by means of spontaneous detachment. It requires insight and study. The *studia humanitatis*, corresponding to our humanities, led to an awareness of what man should be. By means of study, the nature of man, what man truly is, was being discovered and experienced. In many respects it was characteristic of humanist thought that it should reach man through books and through language. The art of printing, as we know, had an immense influence. For many it was almost a miracle (Rabelais spoke of a divine revelation) that they had books and the wisdom contained in them at their immediate disposal in their own surroundings. Is it surprising that they attached such immense importance to books? The world and mankind could be influenced and changed by books. Perhaps it was an illusion, but what a grand illusion! Petrarch lived surrounded by manuscripts, the texts he was reading or writing. Even Machiavelli spent much of his time in this way, despite his active concern with material political problems. And Erasmus even more so, while Montaigne's withdrawal to his tower was a withdrawal to his books.

It is this cohesion of study, insight, life and writing, that makes it so hard for us to appreciate that for the humanists there was no dichotomy between nature and culture. Much has been said about Renaissance realism and even about Renaissance naturalism as if these did not exist before! All we can say about this is probably that the art of that time created a 'nature' and a 'reality' which have largely determined our own views. It follows that just as we have a 'feeling' for the sense of nature in Alberti or Aeneas Piccolimini (who later became Pope Pius II), we continue to think the works of art 'natural' too. But they need not for that reason be more natural than many others which portrayed nature and reality in their own way, and anyway as works of art they could obviously never be nature itself. And this means that even the very 'natural' nature of the Renaissance contained a cultural component. This may well be acceptable as far as art is concerned; it is more difficult to appreciate that to the humanists life itself was a kind of work of art. And yet this is the only way to explain their concept of 'culture'. For in this culture, which is the mark of a cultivated man, or rather, what he should be, the entirety of being human would finally be made manifest. In a constant equilibrium he would experience all physical and spiritual qualities, harmoniously uniting in the totality of his life. One particular form of humanism envisaged this type of man and as such it had literally become an art of living.

One could describe this as mundane humanism, taking 'mundane' in the modern sense of the word. In this sense it is apparent in Castiglione and Montaigne, and certainly in Erasmus too, if cast in a slightly different form. And if 'mundane' is taken to mean not so much 'worldly' and 'frivolous', as 'appertaining to the world in which we live', then this mundane humanism is really common to everyone during that period. Certainly the Platonic thinkers do not deny it, taking it rather for granted and moving from there to the spiritual ascent to God. Others, on the other hand, while not denying such human potentialities, suffer (like Erasmus) from a certain timidity or (like Montaigne) from a certain inability to aspire to this kind of exaltation, and so they confine themselves to the art of living itself. But among all the humanists the communal conviction prevails that man can form himself and the world.

Since this creative potential pulses right through humanism we cannot ignore the religious connotations which this word 'create' must have had at the time. It is highly significant that it was the Renaissance that moved from making to creating. In spite of all the rules of art which had to be learned and applied, it was at this time that they developed the concept of the divinely inspired artist who in his turn, like the god on earth into whom he could grow, was creating works of art. Man as creature and as creation at the same time – here lies the duality which is manifest in all humanist treatises and which is portrayed by the Renaissance. It contains the tension and the harmonious resolution described by each of these scholars in his own way and despite the summits of their achievements in thought and art, herein also lies their deficiency.

It has been observed that humanism, during the sixteenth century in particular, became stifled under conflicting forces. Calvinism and the Council of Trent seem to have snuffed out a way of thinking that wanted to hold fast to a kind of fundamental unity transcending all parties. I also added that Erasmian humanism in particular lost its original identity, but that it seeped through nevertheless and its far-reaching influence can be felt to this day. Now, moreover, it will be clear that this tense, ambivalent thought will never really be able to come to its own fruition; it must inevitably be interrupted by outward circumstances. Driven by the need to create it continues and remains in motion, and even if the soul were temporarily united with God, it would fall back to earth and revert to matter. And there it will dwell

in an atmosphere of nostalgia and melancholy, only to strive once again after detachment and release from life. Some of Michelangelo's figures are the peerless expressions of this uncompleted and endless journey. Nor for that matter, can the journey of mundane humanism ever reach its end either. It too must always go on, constantly reflecting anew. Montaigne's work too remains incomplete and endless. Humanism saw man as god on earth. He is creature and creator. In his own way he can complete a human task, but he must for ever begin his work of completion again.

Chronology

This brief chronology, presented in three sections, is not meant to be in any way complete but to give a skeleton of events specially relevant to the text. Most Latin and some vernacular titles have been translated into English.

Italy

	Philosophy and literature	Fine arts and other events
1300		Giotto working in Assisi and Rome
1304–21	Dante Alighieri, *Divine Comedy*	
1341	Petrarch crowned with the laurel	
1347–51		Black Death devastates Europe
1348–53	Boccaccio, *Decameron*	
1354–7		Orcagna, altar of the Strozzi Chapel, S. Maria Novella, Florence
1375	Salutati appointed Latin Secretary of Florence	
1378		Great Schism begins. Half Europe follows Urban vi and half Clement vii
1380–1400	Salutati, *On the Secular and the Religious*, *On the Labours of Hercules*, *On Fate and Fortune*	
1396	Chrysoloras introduces Greek in Florence	
1405	Bruni, first translations of Plato	
1409		Council of Pisa. (Benedict xiii and Gregory xii deposed; Alexander v elected Pope; rivalry of three Popes)
1414–18		Council of Constance,
1416		Donatello, *St George*, and work on Florence Cathedral

Philosophy and literature	**Fine arts and other events**
1417 Bruni translates Aristotle	
1420–43	Brunelleschi builds cupola of Florence Cathedral, rebuilds S. Lorenzo, and builds a chapel near S. Croce
1431–49	Council of Basel
1434–64	Cosimo de' Medici, founds Medicean rule in Florence
1438 Plethon, as a spokesman for the Eastern Church, arrives in Italy with his pupil Bessarion	
1439 Valla, *On the Freedom of the Will*	Council of Ferrara moves to Florence
1440 Nicholas of Cusa, *On Learned Ignorance*. Bracciolini, *On Nobility*. Platonic Academy founded in Florence. John Gutenberg invents art of printing by movable type	
1447	Accession of Pope Nicholas V
1448–50 Valla writing *Notes on the New Testament*; completes the *Elegantiae*	
1452 Manetti, *On the Dignity and Excellence of Man*	Piero della Francesca, paints murals in Arezzo. Alberti, *On Architecture*
1453	In Rome, republican conspiracy against papal rule
1455 Poggio, *On the Misery of the Human Condition*	
1457 Ficino, *De voluptate*	
1458 Landino starts lecturing at the Studio	
1459 Ficino begins his study of Greek. Argyropoulos starts teaching Greek in Florence	

	Philosophy and literature	Fine arts and other events
1462–8	Ficino translating Plato	
1463	Ficino translates Pimander	
1469	Bessarion, *Against Plato's Opponent*	Lorenzo de' Medici becomes ruler of Florence
1470		Alberti builds façade of S. Maria Novella, Florence
1473	Lorenzo de' Medici, *Altercazione*	
1474		Mantegna, frescoes in the Camera degli Sposi, Mantua
1475	Landino, *On True Nobility*	
1477	Ficino, *On the Christian Religion*	
1478		Botticelli, *Primavera*. Conspiracy of the Pazzi against Medicean rule in Florence
1480	Politian starts lecturing at the Studio	
1481–3		Botticelli, Ghirlandaio, Perugino, Pinturicchio, Signorelli and others paint frescoes in the Sistine Chapel; Leonardo, *Adoration of the Magi* and *Virgin of the Rocks*
1483–4	Publication of Ficino's translation of Plato	
1486	Pico, *On the Dignity of Man*	
1487	Ficino, *Platonic Theology, Concerning the Immortality of the Soul* (written in 1474)	
1489	Politian, *Miscellany*. Pico, *Heptaplus*. Ficino, *On the Threefold Life*	
1491	Pico, *On Being and the One*. Disputation of Cardinal Cajetano and Pico	Savonarola elected prior of San Marco, Florence
1492	Ficino, Latin translation of Plotinus	

Philosophy and literature	Fine arts and other events
1493 Ficino, *On the Sun and Light*	
1494 Pico, *Disputations on Predictive Astrology*. Venetian press of Aldus Manutius issues its first book	
1494–5	Charles VIII of France invades Italy; expulsion of the Medici from Florence; Holy League expels Charles from Italy
1495 Boiardo, *Orlando innamorato*	
1495–7	Leonardo, *Last Supper*
1496 Ficino's commentary on Plato and his translation of Dionysius the Areopagite	
1498	Execution of Savonarola. Machiavelli appointed Secretary of Florence (until 1512)
1500 Aldus founds Venice Academy for the study of Greek, and invents italic type	
1501–4	Michelangelo, *David*
1503	Leonardo, *Mona Lisa*
1504 Sannazaro, *Arcadia*	Giorgione, *Madonna* at Castlelfranco
1505 Bembo, *Gli asolani*	
1505–7	Dürer in Italy
1506	Bramante begins to rebuild St Peter's
1508–12	Michelangelo, frescoes for the Sistine Chapel
1509–11	Raphael, frescoes for the Stanza della Segnatura in the Vatican
1512	Medici restored to power in Florence
1513 Machiavelli, *The Prince*	Correggio, *Virgin with St Francis*. Francis I invades Italy

Philosophy and literature	Fine arts and other events
1516 Ariosto, *Orlando furioso*. Pomponazzi, *On the Immortality of the Soul*	Raphael, Sistine *Madonna*
1518	Titian, *The Assumption of the Virgin*
1520 Machiavelli, *Art of War*; Pomponazzi, *On Fate, Free Will and Predestination*	
1520–34	Michelangelo in Florence, working notably on the Medici tomb chapel and the Biblioteca Laurenziana
1525 Equicola, *On the Nature of Love*	Battle of Pavia: Francis I taken prisoner
1528 Castiglione, *The Courtier*	
1530 Bembo, *Rime*	Correggio, *Adoration of the Shepherds*
1534–41	Michelangelo, *Last Judgment*
1535 Leone Ebreo, *Dialogues on Love*	
1545 Cardano, *Ars magna*	Council of Trent opens
1547	Council of Trent moves to Bologna. Michelangelo appointed chief architect of St Peter's
1550	Vasari, *Lives of the Painters*
1557 Cardano, *On the Variety of Things*	
1570	Palladio, *Treatise on Architecture*
1585 Bruno, *Degli heroici furori*	

Erasmus' life and works

1469   Erasmus born at Deventer

1478   At Deventer with the Brethren of the Common Life

1487   Enters the monastery at Steyn; studies the classics; much impressed by Valla's *Elegantiae*

1495   In Paris at the Collège de Mantaigu; writes first *Colloquies* as textbook of conversation for pupils

1499   First visit to England; meets More and Colet

1500   In Paris; first edition of the *Adages* (838 proverbs)

1502   In Louvain; first translations from Greek

1503   First publication of the *Enchiridion*

1505   Second visit to England

1506   In Italy; doctorate in theology at Turin

1508   New edition of the *Adages* published by Aldus (3260 proverbs)

1509   Leaves Italy for England; writes the *Praise of Folly* at the home of More

1511   Publication of the *Praise of Folly* in Paris. Erasmus settles in Cambridge

1514   In Louvain and Basel

1515   New edition of the *Adages* published by Froben (3411 proverbs)

1516   Publication of *Education of a Christian Prince* (for Charles v). Edition of the New Testament (first Greek text ever printed), and of Jerome, published by Froben

1517   In Louvain till 1521, helping to establish the Collegium Trilingue. Invitation from Francis i to settle in France

1518   English translation (by Tyndale?) of the *Enchiridion*. First (unauthorised) edition of the *Colloquies* by Froben

1519   Erasmus non-committal towards Luther, but under increasing pressure to show his colours

1521   Erasmus considers writing an attack on Luther. Leaves Louvain for good to go to Basel, where he publishes the works of many of the Church Fathers

1522   New enlarged edition of the *Colloquies* published by Froben

1524   *On the Freedom of the Will*, attacking Luther

1526	*Hyperaspistes*, in answer to Luther's reply. *Colloquies* and other writings formally censured by the Sorbonne
1528	*Ciceronianus*, dialogue against the adulation of Cicero
1529	Erasmus leaves Basel for Freiburg
1533	Last edition of the *Adages* during lifetime
1534	Declines cardinalate offered by Pope Paul III; writes *Harmony of the Church*
1535	Returns to Basel
1536	Death of Erasmus in Basel

France : philosophy, literature and fine arts

1470	Fichet writes on rhetoric, acquaints Paris with the work of the Italian humanists, and introduces printing to the Sorbonne
1472	Fichet settles in Rome
1473	Gaguin, Fichet's pupil, continues his work, incorporating the rules of Latin prosody in his teaching programme; corresponds with Ficino
1490	Lefèvre publishes an introduction to Aristotle
1494	Lefèvre publishes hermetic writings in Ficino's translation
1499	Lefèvre publishes Dionysius the Areopagite
1509	Lefèvre writes a commentary on five Latin psalm translations (*Quintuplex Psalterium*)
1510	Bovillus, *Liber de sapiente*
1512	Lefèvre's translation and commentary on St Paul's Epistles
1514	Budé, *De asse et partibus eius* (on ancient coins and antiquities in general). Lefèvre publishes a large edition of Nicholas of Cusa
1515	Leonardo arrives in France. Jean Clouet appointed court painter
1517	Francis I appoints *lecteurs royaux*, to teach Greek and Hebrew (as well as other subjects); tries to persuade Erasmus to come to France
1518	Marot appointed *valet de chambre* to Marguerite of Navarre

1519   Extensions to Chambord castle

1521   Lefèvre publishes a French translation of the Psalms and the New Testament

1522   Budé appointed royal librarian

1524   Lefèvre, translation of the Gospels

1528   Foundations of Fontainebleau castle laid

1529   Budé, *Commentaires sur la langue grecque*

1530   Collège de France founded. Repeated invitation to Erasmus. Marot's first Latin translation: part of Ovid's *Metamorphoses*

1531   Marguerite of Navarre, *Miroir de l'âme pécheresse*. Arrival of Italian painters Il Rosso and Primatticcio in France

1532   Rabelais, *Pantagruel*

1534   Olivetan's translation of the Bible in collaboration with des Périers. Rabelais, *Gargantua*. Robert Estienne, *Thesaurus latinae linguae*

1535   Dolet, *De imitatione ciceroniana*, directed against Erasmus. Budé, *De transitu hellenismi ad christianum*

1536   Calvin, *Institutio religionis christianae*. Dolet, *Commentaires sur la langue latine*

1537   des Périers, *Cymbalum mundi*

1538   Marot, *Oeuvres*. Postel, *De originibus seu de hebraicae linguae et gentis antiquitate*

1539   Postel appointed professor of mathematics and oriental languages at the Collège de France

1540   Arrival of the architect Serlio in France. Cellini at the French court (until 1545). François Clouet succeeds his father as *peintre du Roi*

1541   Calvin publishes French translation of the *Institutio*. Marot translates Psalms.

1542–4   Marguerite of Navarre starts work on the *Heptameron* (it is unfinished at her death)

1544   Founding of the library at Fontainebleau, directed by Vegetius. Dolet translates dialogues of Plato. Scève, *Délie, objet de plus hault vertu* (written for Pernette du Guillet)

1545   Pernette du Guillet, *Oeuvres*

1546	Rabelais, *Tiers livre*. Jean Goujon appointed *sculpteur du Roi*
1547	Marguerite of Navarre, *Comédie jouée à Mont-de-Marsan*
1549	du Bellay, *Défense et illustration de la langue française*, and *Olive*
1550	Ronsard, *Odes*
1555	Ramus, *Dialectique* (first philosophical treatise in French). Ronsard, *Hymnes*. Publication of Louise Labé's works
1557	Ronsard, *Amours*
1558	du Bellay, *Les Regrets*, *Antiquités de Rome*
1559	Amyot's translation of Plutarch; returns to this work in 1572
1562	Scève, *Microcosme*
1566	Henri Estienne, *Traité de la conformité du langage français avec le grec*. Bodin, *The Easy Way to learn History*
1571	Montaigne retires to Bordeaux
1572	Henri Estienne, *Thesaurus graecae linguae*. Ronsard, *La Franciade*
1576	Bodin, *De la république*
1580	Montaigne, *Essais* (two books). Bodin, *Démonomanie*
1588	Montaigne, *Essais* (three books)
1592	Bodin writes *Heptaplomeres*

Bibliography

The following is a selection from a large number of studies. Moreover, all historical journals publish one or more articles on humanism or the Renaissance every year. Since it is impossible to list all these journals I have confined myself to the following:

Archivio di Filosofia (*AF*), *Bibliothèque d'Humanisme et Renaissance* (*BHR*), *Studies in the Renaissance*, *Journal of the History of Ideas* (*JHI*), *Journal of the Warburg and Courtauld Institutes* (*JWCI*)

General

~ Burckhardt, J., *Die Kultur der Renaissance in Italien*, 1860. (Later editions and translations including *The Civilisation of the Renaissance in Italy* translated from the second German edition by S. G. C. Middlemore, London and New York, 1960.)

Chastel, A., *Art et humanisme à Florence au temps de Laurent le Magnifique*, Paris, 1959.

Chastel, A. et Klein, R., *L'âge de l'humanisme*, Paris, 1963 (tr. by Katherine M. Delavenay and E. M. Gwyer), London, 1963 and New York, 1964.

Febvre, L. et Martin, H. J., *L'apparition du livre*, Paris, 1958.

Garin, E., *Italian Humanism*, New York, 1966.
Medioevo e Rinascimento, Bari, 1954.
La cultura filosofica del Rinascimento italiano, Florence, 1961.

+ Highet, G., *The Classical Tradition*, New York and London, 1949.

Kristeller, P. O., *Studies in Renaissance Thought and Letters*, Rome, 1956.
+ *Renaissance Thought I; the Classic, Scholastic and Humanistic Strains*, New York, 1961.
+ *Renaissance Thought II; Papers on Humanism and the Arts*, New York, 1965.

+ Martin, A. von, *Sociology of the Renaissance*, tr. by W. L. Leutkens, London and New York, 1944.

248

Renaudet, A., *Humanisme et Renaissance*, Geneva, 1958.

Rice, E. F., *The Renaissance Idea of Wisdom*, Cambridge, Mass., 1958 and London, 1959.

Saitta, G., *Il pensiero italiano nell'umanesimo e nel Rinascimento*, Bologna, 1949–51.

− Schevill, F., *The Medici*, New York and Gloucester, Mass., 1960.
History of Florence; from the Founding of the City through the Renaissance, New York, 1936.
Pensée humaniste et tradition chrétienne, aux XVe et XVIe siècles, Paris, 1951.
The Renaissance, New York, 1953.

1 Italian humanism

Allers, R., 'Microcosmus from Anaximandros to Paracelsus' in *Traditio* vol. II, New York, 1944.

Anagnine, E., *Pico della Mirandola*, Bari, 1937.

+ Baker, H., *The Image of Man*, New York, 1961.

Baron, H., 'Cicero and the Roman Civic Spirit' *Bulletin of the John Rylands Library*, 1938.

Bezold, F. von, *Das Fortleblen der antiken Gotter*, Bonn and Leipzig, 1922.

− Blunt, A., *Artistic Theory in Italy*, London and New York, 1961.

− Bolgar, R. R., *The Classical Heritage and its Beneficiaries*, London and New York, 1954.

Buck, A., *Italienische Dichtungslehren*, Tübingen, 1952.

+ Cassirer, E., *Individual and the Cosmos in Renaissance Philosophy*, New York and Oxford, 1964.
'Giovanni Pico della Mirandola' in *JHI*, 1942.

+ Cassirer, E. and others, eds., *The Renaissance Philosophy of Man*, Chicago, 1948 and London, 1949.

Courcelle, P., *Les lettres grecques en occident*, Paris, 1948.

Doren, A., *Fortuna im Mittelalter und in der Renaissance*, Leipzig, 1924.

Dulles, A., *Princeps Concordiae*, Cambridge, Mass., 1941.

Gombrich, E. H., 'Botticelli's Mythologies', *JWCI*, 1945.
'Icones Symbolicae', *JWCI*, 1948.

Jaeger, W., *Humanistische Reden und Vortrage*, Berlin and Leipzig, 1960.

Klein, R., 'Les humanistes et la science', *BHR*, 1961.

Klibansky, R., Saxl, F. and Panofsky, E.. *Saturn and Melancholy* (Studies in the History of Natural Philosophy), Edinburgh and London, 1964.

Kristeller, P. O., *The Philosophy of Marsilio Ficino*, New York, 1953.

Liebeschütz, H., *Fulgentius Metaforalis*, Leipzig, 1926.

Marcel, R., *Marsile Ficin*, Paris, 1958.

Newald, R., *Nachleben des antiken Geistes*, Tübingen, 1960.

Panofsky, E., *Die Perspektive als symbolische Form*, Leipzig and Berlin, 1924.

Panofsky, E. and Saxl F., 'Classical Mythology in Medieval Art, *Metropolitan Museum Studies*, 1939.

Pépin, J., *Mythe et allégorie* (coll. 'Philosophie de l'esprit'), Paris, 1958.

Ruegg, W., *Cicero und der Humanismus*, Zurich, 1946.

Secret, F., *Les kabbalistes chrétiens de la Renaissance*, Paris, 1964.
· *Le Zohâr chez les kabbalistes chrétiens de la Renaissance* (coll. 'Etudes-Juives'), The Hague and Paris, 1964.

+ Seznec, J., *The Survival of the Pagan Gods*, (Bollingen Series), New York and London, 1953; Gloucester, Mass., 1961.

Walker, D. P., 'Orpheus the Theologian and Renaissance Platonists', *JWCI*, 1953.
Spiritual and Demonic Magic from Ficino to Campanella, (Warburg Institute Studies, vol. 22), London, 1958.

Weinberg, B., *A History of Literary Criticism in the Renaissance*, Chicago, 1961.
+ Wind, E., *Pagan Mysteries in the Renaissance*, New Haven and London, 1958.
Wittkower, R., *Architectural Principles in the Age of Humanism*, London, 1949 and 1952; New York, 1965.

Each of the following is a collection of articles by various contributors to *AF*: 'Testi umanistici su la retorica', *AF*, 1953; 'Testi umanistici su l'ermetismo' *AF*, 1955; 'Umanesimo e esoterismo', *AF*, 1960.

2 Erasmus

+ Huizinga, J., *Erasmus*, New York, 1924, London, 1952.
Margolin, J. C., *Érasme par lui-meme*, Paris, 1965.
Oelrich, K. H., *Der späte Erasmus und die Reformation*, Munster-Westfalen, 1961.
Pfeiffer, R., *Humanitas Erasmiana*, Leipzig, 1931.
+ Phillips, M. M., *The Adages of Erasmus*, London and New York, 1964.
Renaudet, A., *Études Érasmiennes*, Paris, 1939.
Érasme et l'Italie, Paris, 1955.
– Smith, P., *Erasmus*, New York, 1923.
+ Thompson, C. R. (tr.), *The Colloquies of Erasmus*, London and Chicago, 1965.

3 Humanism and French literature

Bohatec, J., *Budé und Calvin*, Graz, 1950.
Busson, H., *Le rationalisme dans la littérature française* (coll. De Pétrarque à Descartes), Paris, 1957.

Cantimori, D., *Italienische Haeretiker der Spätrenaissance*, Basel, 1949.

Eritici italiani del cinquecento, ricerche, storiche, Florence, 1939.

Castor, G., *Pléiade Poetics*, New York and London, 1964.

Chamard, H., *Histoire de la Pléiade*, Paris, 1939.

Febvre, L., *Le problème de l'incroyance au XVIe siècle*, Paris, 1947.

Au coeur religieux du XVIe siècle, Paris, 1957.

Origène et des Périers, Paris, 1942.

Autour de l'Héptaméron, Paris, 1957.

Festugière, J., *La philosophie de l'amour de Marsile Ficin*, Graz and Paris, 1941.

Jung, E. M., 'On the Nature of Evangelism in Sixteenth-Century Italy', *JHI*, 1953.

Mann, M., *Érasme et les débuts de la Réforme française*, (*1517–1536*), Paris, 1934.

Mesnard, P., *L'essor de la philosophie politique au XVIe siècle*, Paris, 1951.

Moore, W. G., *La Réforme allemande et la littérature française*, Strasbourg, 1930.

Renaudet, A., *Préréforme et humanisme à Paris*, Paris, 1953.

Saulnier, V-L., 'Le sens du Cymbalum Mundi', *BHR*, 1951.

Le dessein de Rabelais, Paris, 1957.

Maurice Scève, Paris, 1949.

Schmidt, A-M., *La poésie scientifique en France au XVIe siècle*, Paris, 1938.

Screech, M. A., *L'évangélisme de Rabelais*, Geneva, 1959.

Simone, F., *Il Rinascimento francese*, 1961.

Walker, D. P., 'The Prisca Theologia in France', *JWCI*, 1954.

Weber, H., *La création poétique au XVIe siècle en France*, Paris, 1956.

Yates, Frances A., *French Academies of the Sixteenth Century*, New York and London, 1947.

4 Montaigne and the adventure

Bouwsma, W. J., *Concordia Mundi – the Career and Thought of Guillaume Postel*, Cambridge, Mass., 1957 and London, 1958.

Friedrich, H., *Montaigne*, Berne, 1949.

Sclafert, C., *L'âme religieuse de Montaigne*, Paris, 1951.

Traeger, W. E., *Aufbau und Gedankenführung in Montaignes Essays*, Heidelberg, 1961.

Yates, Frances A., *Giordano Bruno and the Hermetic Tradition*, London and Chicago, 1964.

5 Renaissance and humanism

Campana, A., 'The origin of the word "humanist",' *JWCI*, 1946.

Ferguson, W. K., *The Renaissance in Historical Thought*, New York, 1948.

Fliche, A. and others, *Quelques aspects de l'humanisme médiéval*, Montpellier, 1943.

+ Haskins, Ch. H., *The Renaissance of the Twelfth Century*, New York, 1957.

Panofsky, E., *Renaissance and Renascences in Western Art*, New York, 1960 and Stockholm, 1961.

Renucci, P., *L'aventure de l'humanisme européen au moyen âge*, Paris, 1953.

Ullman, B. L., 'Renaissance – the Word and the Underlying Concept', *Studies in Philology*, 1952.

Index

254

World University Library

Already published

Eye and Brain
R. L. Gregory, *Cambridge*

**The Economics of
Underdeveloped Countries**
Jagdish Bhagwati, *Dehli*

The Left in Europe since 1789
David Caute, *Oxford*

The World Cities
Peter Hall, *London*

Chinese Communism
Robert North, *Stanford*

**The Emergence of Greek
Democracy**
W. G. Forrest, *Oxford*

The Quest for Absolute Zero
K. Mendelssohn, *Oxford*

The Biology of Work
O. G. Edholm, *London*

Palaeolithic Cave Art
P. J. Ucko and A. Rosenfeld, *London*

Particles and Accelerators
Robert Gouiran, *C E R N, Geneva*

**Russian Writers and Society
1825–1904**
Ronald Hingley, *Oxford*

Words and Waves
A. H. W. Beck, *Cambridge*

Education in the Modern World
John Vaizey, *London*

The Rise of Toleration
Henry Kamen, *Warwick*

Art Nouveau
S. Tschudi Madsen, *Oslo*

The World of an Insect
Rémy Chauvin, *Strasbourg*

**Decisive Forces in World
Economics**
J. L. Sampedro, *Madrid*

Development Planning
Jan Tinbergen, *Rotterdam*

Human Communication
J. L. Aranguren, Madrid

Mathematics Observed
H. Freudenthal, *Utrecht*

The Rise of the Working Class
Jürgen Kuczynski, *Berlin*

The Science of Decision-making
A. Kaufmann, *Paris*

Chinese Medicine
P. Huard and M. Wong, *Paris*

**Muhammad and the
Conquests of Islam**
Francesco Gabrieli, *Rome*